LET NOTHING TROUBLE YOU

The Saints Speak Today Series

Let Nothing Trouble You
St. Teresa of Avila

Restless Till We Rest in You
St. Augustine

A Dwelling Place Within
St. Francis of Assisi (available April 1999)

Be Merry in God
St. Thomas More (available April 1999)

THE SAINTS SPEAK TODAY

Let Nothing Trouble You

60 Reflections from the Writings of
Teresa of Avila

COMPILED BY
HEIDI S. HESS

CHARIS
SERVANT PUBLICATIONS
ANN ARBOR, MICHIGAN

Charis Books is an imprint of Servant Publications especially designed to serve Roman
Catholics.

This work is based on excerpts from *The Collected Works of St. Teresa of Avila,*
volumes 1–3, translated by Kieran Kavanaugh, O.C.D. and Otilio Rodriguez, O.C.D.
The publisher wishes to thank ICS Publications (Washington, D.C.) for their
cooperation in the completion of this project.

Quotes from *The Letters of Saint Teresa of Jesus,* are from the edition translated by E.
Allison Peers. © 1951, 1980 by Burns and Oates Ltd. Printed in Great Britain, for
Sheed and Ward Ltd., London by Bidles Ltd., Guilford, Surrey. All rights reserved.
Used by permission.

Servant Publications
P.O. Box 8617
Ann Arbor, MI 48107

Cover design: Left Coast Design, Inc., Portland, OR

98 99 00 01 10 9 8 7 6 5 4 3 2 1

Printed in the United States of America
ISBN 1-56955-062-X

CIP information on file with the Library of Congress

*F*or my goddaughter, Emily Jane.
May you come to know God as intimately
as St. Teresa did.

To her mother, Elizabeth Milne,
who labored patiently with me to complete this project,
and Bill Hardison and Dave Hudgins
for their technical expertise and support:
Your friendships have been golden gifts.

And to the rest of my family and friends,
who have encouraged me
to follow His Majesty, wherever He may lead.

CONTENTS

*L*et nothing trouble you,
Let nothing frighten you,
All is fleeting,
God alone is unchanging.
Patience everything obtains.
Who possesses God
Wants for nothing.
God alone suffices.

Adapted from "Efficacy of Patience"
from Teresa of Avila's *Poetry*

INTRODUCTION

"*Let nothing trouble you....*" These were the words of a sixteenth-century Spanish noblewoman-turned-nun who spoke with conviction born of experience.

At first we might be tempted to brush aside her admonition. After all, the experiences of St. Teresa were very different from our own: Driven by our frenetic schedules, we dash off to Sunday Mass, pray the occasional Rosary when our world spins off course, and observe the annual relinquishment of some mild luxury in the name of Lent. What relevant insights could this sixteenth-century mystic offer us today?

I invite you to take a closer look. Christians in every time and place have faced the same struggles: times of weakness, the death of some cherished dream, the niggling reminder of some personal failure, or the soul-searing effect of a certain temptation we cannot seem to shake. We may turn to friends and family for support and reassurance, or somehow try to insulate ourselves from the painful reality of our struggle. And yet we can never quite get away from ourselves.

An examination of St. Teresa's life reveals a woman who understood true hardship. And yet she always refused to take the easy way or to shield herself from the real world. Instead, she looked *beyond* this present reality to a deeper, more lasting dimension. The writings of Teresa of Avila are a treasure map by which we can find the way to the throne room where His Majesty (St. Teresa's name for God) resides. When life closes in around us, it is here that we most need to be.

About St. Teresa

Teresa of Avila (1515–82) was born to devout parents, and enjoyed a happy childhood until her mother died when St. Teresa was fourteen. Soon after, the young Spanish noblewoman was sent to Our Lady of Grace convent in Avila, which was run by Augustinian nuns. Wealthy young women in St. Teresa's day were frequently shunted off to convents for safekeeping, whether or not they truly had a vocation. Since at that time this was the only respectable alternative to marriage, convents were filled with young women who enjoyed a life of relative ease and few responsibilities. Their family's money insulated these women from the rigors of spiritual pursuit.

However, even as a child St. Teresa showed an unusual capacity for spiritual things, and in time decided that God had given her a vocation. Her father was initially opposed to her becoming a nun, and it was not until the age of twenty that she managed to leave her father's home and go to the Carmelite Convent of the Incarnation.

A beautiful, intelligent woman, St. Teresa struggled with both vanity and self-doubt. She endured protracted periods of illness—some attribute it to malaria—and discovered the healing power of prayer when the doctors claimed that they could do no more for her. As she got better, however, her prayer life took a turn for the worse. In time St. Teresa realized that if she was going to achieve true spiritual intimacy, she had to relinquish all personal and social attachments. *Detachment, with humility* ... these two virtues are at the very heart of the life and writings of this dear lady of Avila.

St. Teresa faced nearly half a century of infirmity, adversity, and periodic self-doubt from the time she entered religious life until her death at the age of sixty-seven. Though she was naturally bright and charming, her deep desire for personal holiness and spiritual intimacy with God made her an object of ridicule and censure among those who were content with the spiritual status quo. The austerity of the reforms she introduced to her religious community forced St. Teresa to withstand the suspicion and prejudice most prophetic voices must endure. And yet by her obedience and uncompromising virtue, St. Teresa encountered the holy, burning passion of God in a way that few have experienced before or since.

The same graces that prompted Teresa to draw near to God's heart inspired her to lead others there as well. This was no simple matter. In sixteenth-century Spain, women mystics had two strikes against them, as neither the feminine nor the mystical were warmly regarded. As Teresa herself observed:

When You walked in the world, [You did not] despise women; rather, You always, with great compassion, helped them.... Since the world's judges are sons of Adam and all of them men, there is no virtue in women that they do not hold suspect. Yes, indeed, the day will come, my King, when everyone will be known for what he is. I do not speak for myself, because the world already knows my wickedness ... but because I see that these are times in which it would be wrong to undervalue virtuous and strong souls, even though they are women.[1]

Teresa undoubtedly felt the limitations of her sex, but was not bound by them. It is highly unlikely that she received any formal theological training, as both the publication and reading of Scripture in the vernacular were forbidden in her day.[2] This makes her knowledge and use of the Scriptures as well as her keen insights into deep spiritual truth even more remarkable.

Armed with nothing but her winning charm, her gift of leadership, and her reputation, she brought sweeping reform to the Carmelite order. Though at first she tried to bring about reform from within the existing order, she ultimately obtained permission from Rome to form a new order that was subject to a simpler, more pious rule. The Discalced ("Shoeless") Carmelites received final approval from Rome in 1580. At the time of her death in 1582, St. Teresa had founded seventeen houses.

St. Teresa's work within the Carmelite order alone might have caused her to be considered a leader in the Catholic Reformation. However, her greatest contributions to Catholic spirituality are those she penned in her quieter moments, often under obedience to her superiors. She wrote *The Way of Perfection* and her *Foundations* primarily for the direction and edification of her sisters, but they may be read with benefit by anyone who seeks to deepen their prayer life. *The Interior Castle*, her best-known work, uses vivid images—gardens, silkworms, and diamonds among them—to illustrate the ongoing process of spiritual maturation. *The Book of Her Life*, which was studied and cleared by the Inquisition's censor in 1575, was never returned to St. Teresa in her lifetime, but was ultimately placed in the royal library of King Philip II next to works by St. John Chrysostom and St. Augustine, two doctors of the Church. St. Teresa herself was declared a doctor of the Church by Pope Paul VI in 1970, and her work continues to bring spiritual renewal to many people.

A Guide to *The Interior Castle*

The vivid imagery contained in *The Interior Castle* adds richness and texture to St. Teresa's profound spiritual insights. To explain how a soul matures by drawing deeper into Infinite Love, she compares the human soul to a castle with seven concentric rooms. With great passion she describes how the soul, as it gradually relinquishes both sin and earthly attachments, may draw —and be drawn—ever nearer to His Majesty, who resides in the innermost chamber of the believer's heart.

As I read this work, I was struck by the similarities St. Teresa drew between her pursuit of Infinite Love and the human pursuit of the most intimate of human relationships—marriage. St. Teresa describes spiritual intimacy as a process by which the soul weans itself from all other attachments in order to concentrate on the single most important one. The soul moves from a simple awareness of God (the first room of the chamber), to an increasing attraction that culminates in betrothal (room six) and spiritual marriage and its delights (room seven). Reading St. Teresa's unabashed expressions of love and delight for her Beloved, I was reminded that all human relations reflect, however dimly, the kind of intimacy God longs to have with each of us. And yet, in both spiritual and emotional intimacy, a certain level of detachment and humility is required. We must pass through each stage. There is no rushing the process.

As the soul moves from room to room, it becomes engaged in ever-deepening levels of prayer. As it approaches the seventh chamber, the soul's pursuit of God becomes less active and more passive. The soul simply receives with increasing gratitude and awareness the graces God extends. St. Teresa distinguishes between meditation (the soul focusing its attentions on God) and contemplation (the soul's receiving God's attentions) in order to further emphasize the necessity of surrendering to the Divine Will.

To illustrate the difference between meditation and contemplation, St. Teresa introduces a second image—a garden. This garden may be tended by the gardener in four different ways, each requiring successively less effort from the gardener as the garden grows closer to the Source of the water.[3] As God sends these consolations, moving the soul from simple meditation to true contemplation, the human soul expands as it draws closer to God, and so becomes able to embrace His love even more fully.

The third image, the silkworm, provides an image of perfect detachment, for it is only when the worm has broken free from its cocoon of self-will that the butterfly is free to ascend into the perfect will of God.

A Final Word

St. Teresa's works have touched the lives of millions of men and women, both lay and religious, challenging them to seek deeper intimacy with God with courage, humility, and resolve. With eloquence and zeal, St. Teresa encourages us to relinquish the things that stand between God and us, and to delve ever deeper inside the castle of our souls.

St. Teresa points the way for those whose hearts long for something more spiritually satisfying, for the "faith of our fathers," stronger and deeper than what we have yet experienced. So, we draw upon this sister's experience, hoping to find the key to His Majesty's chamber, to discover a source of lasting peace and joy that we may have long overlooked.

Each of the sixty daily reflections contained in this book comprise a morning and evening reading from the writings of St. Teresa. In some cases the language has been slightly adapted or condensed in order to assist your devotional reading. Each daily reading also contains a complementary Scripture passage, a thought for you to ponder throughout the day, and an excerpt from a hymn. While the writers of these hymns did not all profess to be Roman Catholic, the profoundly intimate expressions of faith are among the Church's greatest possessions.

Some days you will find that the pieces are loosely constructed in order to give your mind and spirit "room to breathe." Other times the readings are more focused in order to help you appreciate a particularly important aspect of St. Teresa's writing. However, I hope that each day you will find some grain of truth that will feed your soul and inspire you to resolve, in the words of St. Teresa, to *"let nothing trouble you … God alone suffices."*

Come, Thou Fount …

The Soul's Prayerful Journey

Draw Near to the Fountain

How precious is thy steadfast love, O God!
The children of men take refuge in the shadow of thy wings.
They feast on the abundance of thy house,
and thou givest them drink from the river of thy delights.
For with thee is the fountain of life;
in thy light do we see light.

PSALM 36:7-9

MORNING READING

Let's consider that we see two founts with two water troughs. These two troughs are filled with water in different ways; with one the water comes from far away through many aqueducts and the use of much ingenuity; with the other the source of the water is right there, and the trough fills without any noise. If the spring is abundant, the water overflows once the trough is filled, forming a large stream. There is no need of any skill, nor does the building of aqueducts have to continue; but water is always flowing from the spring.

The water coming from the aqueducts is comparable to the consolations that are drawn from meditation. With this other fount, the water comes from its own source which is God. And since His Majesty desires to do so, He produces this delight with the greatest peace and sweetness in the very interior part of ourselves.

Come, Thou Fount of every blessing, tune my heart
   to sing Thy grace;
Streams of mercy, never ceasing, call for songs of loudest praise.
Teach me some melodious sonnet, sung by flaming tongues above;
Praise the mount—I'm fixed upon it—mount of God's
   redeeming love.

ROBERT ROBINSON, 1758

FOR REFLECTION

Lord, show me how to draw closer to the fountain of grace that
flows from Your sacred heart.

EVENING READING

There was a well with very bad water according to those who tried
it, and it seemed impossible for the water to flow since the well
was very deep. When I called some workmen to dig a new one,
they laughed at me as though I were wanting to throw money
away. I asked the Sisters what they thought. One said that it
should be tried, that since our Lord would have to provide
someone to bring us water as well as food, it would be cheaper for
His Majesty to give us the well on the grounds of the house and
that thus He would not fail to do so. Observing the great faith
and determination with which she said it, I became certain. And,
contrary to the opinion of the one who understood all about
founts and water, I went ahead. And the Lord was pleased that we
were able to put in a conduit which provided water for our needs,
and for drinking, and which we now have. *[Editor's note: The
"miracle well" exists to this day, and bears testimony to God's ability
to provide for our physical as well as spiritual needs.]*

DAY 2
The Four Waters of God's Abundance

Thou makest springs gush forth in the valleys;
they flow between the hills,
they give drink to every beast of the field....
From thy lofty abode thou waterest the mountains;
the earth is satisfied with the fruit of thy work.

PSALM 104:10, 13

MORNING READING

It has been explained how the garden is watered by drawing water from the well. Let us speak now of the second manner, ordained by the Lord of the garden, for getting water; that is, by turning the crank of a water wheel and by aqueducts, the gardener obtains more water with less labor. Here the soul begins to be recollected and comes upon something supernatural because in no way can it acquire this prayer through any efforts it may make. The water is higher, and so the labor is much less. In this prayer the faculties are gathered within so as to enjoy that satisfaction with greater delight.

Let us come now to speak of the third way by which this garden is irrigated, that is, the water flowing from a river or spring. By this means the garden is irrigated with much less labor, although some labor is required to direct the flow of the water. The Lord so desires to help the gardener here that He Himself becomes practically the gardener and the one who does everything.

This prayer is a sleep of the faculties: the faculties neither fail entirely to function nor understand how they function. The consolation, the sweetness, and the delight are incomparably greater than that experienced in the previous prayer. The water of grace rises up to the throat of this soul since such a soul can no

20

longer move forward; nor does it know how; nor can it move backward.

"There shall be showers of blessing"—this is the promise of love;
There shall be seasons refreshing, sent from the Savior above.
Showers of blessing, showers of blessing we need;
Mercy-drops round us are falling, but for the showers we plead.

DANIEL W. WHITTLE, 1840–1901

FOR REFLECTION

Lord, quench the drought in my soul with the life-giving water of Your Spirit.

EVENING READING

In the previous degrees, the senses are given freedom to show some signs of the great joy they feel. Here in this fourth water the soul rejoices incomparably more; but it can show much less since no power remains in the body, nor does the soul have any power to communicate its joy. What I'm attempting to explain is what the soul feels when it is in this divine union. O infinite Largesse; how magnificent are Your works! That You bestow such sovereign favors on souls that have offended You so much certainly brings my intellect to a halt.

After I have just received these favors, it often happens that I say: *Lord, look what You are doing. Don't forget so quickly my great wickedness. Don't, my Creator, pour such precious liqueur in so broken a bottle; You have already seen at other times how I only spill and waste it. Don't let Your love be so great, eternal King, as to place in risk such precious jewels.* I saw afterward my foolishness and lack of humility; the Lord well knows what is fitting and that I would not have the strength in my soul to be saved if His Majesty didn't give it to me through so many favors.

Prayer Is More Than the Words You Say

When you pray, you must not be like the hypocrites; for they love to stand and pray in the synagogues and at the street corners, that they may be seen by men. Truly, I say to you, they have their reward. But when you pray, go into your room and shut the door and pray to your Father who is in secret; and your Father who sees in secret will reward you.

MATTHEW 6:5-6

MORNING READING

What I would like you to do [when engaged in vocal prayer] is refuse to be satisfied with merely pronouncing the words. For when I say, "I believe," it seems to me right that I should know and understand what I believe. And when I say, "Our Father," it will be an act of love to understand who this Father of ours is and who the Master is who taught us this prayer.

One cannot speak simultaneously to God and to the world; this would amount to nothing more than reciting the prayer while listening to what is being said elsewhere or to letting the mind wander and making no effort to control it.

Sweet hour of prayer, sweet hour of prayer
That calls me from a world of care
And bids me at my Father's throne
Make all my wants and wishes known.
In seasons of distress and grief,
My soul has often found relief,
And oft escaped the tempter's snare
By thy return, sweet hour of prayer.

WILLIAM W. WALFORD, 1772–1850

FOR REFLECTION

"To pray vocally with perfection means that you be aware of and understand whom you are asking, who it is that is asking, and what you are asking for."

Lord, give me a fresh vision of what it means to call you "Father."

EVENING READING

It will happen, when the Lord is pleased, that while the soul is in prayer and very much in its senses a suspension will suddenly be experienced in which the Lord will reveal deep secrets. It seems the soul sees these secrets in God Himself, for they are not visions of the most sacred humanity.

This favor is most beneficial. Even though it passes in a moment, it remains deeply engraved in the soul. The evil of offending God is seen more clearly, because while being in God Himself we commit great evils.

DAY 4

God Delights in the Simple Prayer of a Sincere Soul

For we have not a high priest who is unable to sympathize with our weaknesses, but one who in every respect has been tempted as we are, yet without sinning. Let us then with confidence draw near to the throne of grace, that we may receive mercy and find grace to help in time of need.

HEBREWS 4:15-16

MORNING READING

Because of His humility, the King listens to me and lets me approach Him; and His guards do not throw me out, even though as an uneducated person I don't know how to speak to Him. The angels who assist Him know well the attitude of their King, for He delights more in the unpolished manners of a humble shepherd who He realizes would say more if he knew more than He does in the talk of very wise and learned men, however elegant their discourse, if they don't walk in humility. But just because He is good doesn't mean that we should be rude. At least, in order to thank Him for the bad odor He must endure in consenting to allow one like myself to come near Him, we should strive to be aware of His purity and of who He is.

Oh, our Emperor, supreme Power, supreme Goodness, Wisdom itself, without beginning, without end, without any limit to Your works; they are infinite and incomprehensible, a fathomless sea of marvels, with a beauty containing all beauty, strength itself!

Open my eyes, that I may see glimpses of truth Thou hast for me;
Place in my hands the wonderful key that shall unclasp
*   and set me free.*
Silently now I wait for Thee, ready, my God, Thy will to see;
Open my eyes, illumine me, Spirit divine!

CLARA H. SCOTT, 1895

FOR REFLECTION

Lord, what an awesome privilege it is to come into Your presence!

EVENING READING

Yes, bring yourselves to consider and understand whom you are speaking with, or, as you approach, with whom you are about to speak. In a thousand lives we could never completely understand the way in which this Lord deserves that we speak with Him, for the angels tremble before Him. He commands all; He can do all; for Him, to will is to do.

Well then, it is only right that we try to delight in these grandeurs our Spouse possesses and that we understand whom we are wedded to and what kind of life we must live.

Prayer Exercises the Soul and Brings Other Great Rewards

Therefore I prayed, and understanding was given me;
I called upon God, and the spirit of wisdom came to me....
I loved her more than health and beauty,
And I chose her rather than light,
* because her radiance never ceases.*

WISDOM 7:7, 10

MORNING READING

Souls who do not practice prayer are like people with paralyzed or crippled bodies; even though they have hands and feet they cannot give orders to these hands and feet. Thus there are souls so ill and so accustomed to being involved in external matters that there is no remedy, nor does it seem they can enter within themselves.

If these souls do not strive to understand and cure their great misery, they will be changed into statues of salt, unable to turn their heads to look at themselves, just as Lot's wife was changed for having turned her head.

The King of love my Shepherd is, whose goodness faileth never;
I nothing lack if I am His, and He is mine forever.
In death's dark vale I fear no ill, with Thee, dear Lord, beside me;
Thy rod and staff my comfort still, Thy cross before to guide me.

HENRY W. BAKER, 1821–1877

FOR REFLECTION

"Even though we do not hear Him, He speaks well to the heart when we beseech Him from the heart.... Nor is there any need to shout. However softly we speak, He is near enough to hear us."

EVENING READING

It's an amusing thing that even though we still have a thousand impediments and imperfections and our virtues have hardly begun to grow, we are yet not ashamed to seek spiritual delights in prayer or to complain about dryness. May this never happen to you. Embrace the cross your Spouse has carried and understand that this must be your task.

His Majesty knows best what is suitable for us. There's no need for us to be advising Him about what He should give us, for He can rightly tell us that we don't know what we're asking for. The whole aim of any person who is beginning prayer should be that he work and prepare himself with determination and every possible effort to bring his will into conformity with God's will.

We Must Be Diligent in Seeking the Lord and Responding to His Call

Exhort one another every day, as long as it is called "today," that none of you may be hardened by the deceitfulness of sin. For we share in Christ, if only we hold our first confidence firm to the end, while it is said, "Today, when you hear his voice, do not harden your hearts as in the rebellion."

HEBREWS 3:13-15

MORNING READING

What bride is there who in receiving many valuable jewels from her bridegroom will refuse to give him even a ring, not because of what it is worth, for everything belongs to him, but to give it as a pledge that she will be his until death? Does this Lord deserve less, that we should mock Him by giving and then taking back the trifle that we gave Him? But this little bit of time that we resolve to give Him, which we spend on ourselves and on someone who will not thank us for it, let us give to Him, since we desire to do so, with our thoughts free of other things and unoccupied by them. I should consider the time of prayer as not belonging to me and think that he can ask it of me in justice when I do not want to give it wholly to Him.

Represent the Lord Himself as close to you and behold how lovingly and humbly He is teaching you. Believe me, you should remain with so good a friend as long as you can. If you grow accustomed to having Him present at your side, and He sees that you do so with love and that you go about striving to please Him; He will never fail you; He will help you in all your trials; you will find Him everywhere.

Take time to be holy, be calm in thy soul;
Each thought and each motive beneath His control;
Thus led by His Spirit to fountains of love,
Thou soon shall be fitted for service above.

WILLIAM D. LONGSTAFF, 1882

FOR REFLECTION

"I read in a book that, if we forsake God when He wants us, we shall not find Him when we want Him." Lord, make me sensitive to the promptings of Your Spirit today.

EVENING READING

When we do not give ourselves to His Majesty with the determination with which He gives Himself to us, He does a good deal by leaving us in mental prayer and visiting us from time to time like servants in His vineyard. But these others [who receive the consolations of contemplation] are favored children. He would not want them to leave His side, nor does He leave them, for they no longer want to leave Him. He seats them at His table, He shares with them His food even to the point of taking a portion from His own mouth to give them.

Oh, blessed renunciation of things so small and so base that reaches so high a state. What would it matter, when you are in the arms of God, if the whole world blamed you! He has the power to free you from everything, for once He commanded that the world be made, it was made; His will is the deed.

DAY 7
Hindrances to a Fertile Prayer Life

We beseech you, brethren, to respect those who labor among you and are over you in the Lord and admonish you, and to esteem them very highly in love because of their work. Be at peace among yourselves. And we exhort you, brethren, admonish the idle, encourage the faint-hearted, help the weak, be patient with them all. See that none of you repays evil for evil, but always seek to do good to one another and to all. Rejoice always, pray constantly, give thanks in all circumstances; for this is the will of God in Christ Jesus for you.

1 THESSALONIANS 5:12-18

MORNING READING

Our primitive rule states that we must pray without ceasing. If we do this with all the care possible—for unceasing prayer is the most important aspect of the rule—the fasts, the disciplines, and the silence the order commands will not be wanting. For you already know that if prayer is to be genuine, it must be helped by these other things; *prayer and comfortable living are incompatible.*

O the beautiful treasures laid up for the wise,
How precious the value, how glorious the prize!
Far brighter than diamonds on princes' brow,
And richer than royalty can bestow.
O the beautiful treasures laid up for the wise.

OLD SHAKER HYMN

FOR REFLECTION

Lord, reveal to me whatever is keeping me from loving You without reservation. Give me the courage to relinquish it.

EVENING READING

Take no notice of that feeling you get of wanting to leave off in the middle of your prayer, but praise the Lord for the desire you have to pray: that, you may be sure, comes from your will, which loves to be with God. It is just melancholy that oppresses you and gives you the feeling of constraint. Try occasionally, when you find yourself oppressed in that way, to go to some place where you can see the sky, and walk up and down a little: doing that will not interfere with your prayer, and we must treat this human frailty of ours in such a way that our nature is not subjected to undue constraint. We are seeking God all the time, and it is because of this that we go about in search of means to that end, and it is essential that the soul should be led gently.

Descend Upon My Heart ...

The Soul Learns to Love and Fear the Lord

DAY 8

Love and Fear of the Lord:
The Soul's Sure Defense

In the fear of the Lord one has strong confidence,
And his children will have a refuge.
The fear of the Lord is a fountain of life,
That one may avoid the snares of death.

PROVERBS 14:26-27

MORNING READING

Now, then, Good Master, teach us how to live without any sudden assault in so dangerous a war [which the devil assails upon those who pursue virtue]. What we can have and what His Majesty gave us [for protection] are love and fear. Love will quicken our steps; fear will make us watch our steps to avoid falling along the way. Love and fear of God: what more could you ask for! They are like two fortified castles from which one can wage war on the world and the devils.

Those who truly love God, love every good, desire every good, favor every good, praise every good. They always join, favor, and defend good people. They have no love for anything but truth and whatever is worthy of love. Do you think it is possible for a person who really loves God to love vanities? No, indeed, he cannot; nor can he love riches, or worldly things, or delights, or honors, or strife, or envy. All of this is so because he seeks only to please the Beloved.

34

My Jesus, I love Thee, I know Thou art mine;
For Thee all the follies of sin I resign;
My gracious Redeemer, my Savior art Thou;
If ever I loved Thee, my Jesus, 'tis now.

WILLIAM R. FEATHERSTONE, 1862

FOR REFLECTION

In the words of St. Teresa, "Let me not leave this life, O my Lord, until I no longer desire anything in it; neither let me know any love outside of You, Lord, nor let me succeed in using this term 'love' for anyone else. Everything is false since the foundation is false, and so the edifice doesn't last."

EVENING READING

He told me, "Alas, daughter, how few there are who truthfully love Me! For if they loved Me, I would reveal to them My secrets. Do you know what it is to love Me truthfully? It is to understand that everything that is displeasing to Me is a lie. By the beneficial effects this understanding will cause in your soul, you shall see clearly what you now do not understand."

The Lord Is Patient
in Revealing Himself to Us

I saw the Lord sitting upon a throne, high and lifted up; and his train filled the temple. Above him stood the seraphim; each had six wings: with two he covered his face, with two he covered his feet, and with two he flew. And one called to another and said, "Holy, holy, holy is the Lord of hosts; the whole earth is full of his glory."

ISAIAH 6:1-3

MORNING READING

One day, while I was at prayer, the Lord desired to show me only His hands which were so very beautiful that I would be unable to exaggerate the beauty. This vision caused me great fear; any supernatural favor the Lord grants me frightens me at first, when it is new. After a few days I saw also that divine face which it seems left me completely absorbed. Since afterward He granted me the favor of seeing Him entirely, I couldn't understand why the Lord showed Himself to me in this way, little by little, until later I understood that His Majesty was leading me in accordance with my natural weakness. May He be blessed forever! So much glory would have been unbearable next to so lowly and wretched a subject as I; and as one who knew this, the merciful Lord was preparing me.

Great God of wonders! All Thy ways are matchless,
God-like, and divine;
But the fair glories of Thy grace
more God-like and unrivaled shine...
Who is a pardoning God like Thee?
Or who has grace so rich and free?

SAMUEL DAVIES, 1723–1761

FOR REFLECTION

Let your love embolden me to approach You. Let Your greatness persuade me not to treat You too familiarly.

EVENING READING

O my Lord, how You are the true friend; and how powerful! When You desire You can love, and You never stop loving those who love You! All things praise You, Lord of the world! Oh, who will cry out for You, to tell everyone how faithful You are to Your friends! All things fail; You, Lord of all, never fail.

Happy are those who with the strong fetters and chains of the kindnesses of the mercy of God find themselves prisoners and deprived of the power to break loose. *Love is strong as death, and unyielding as hell.* Short is all life in exchange for Your eternity; very long is one day alone and one hour for those who don't know and who fear whether they will offend You! Oh, when will that happy day arrive when you will see yourself drowned in the infinite sea of supreme truth, where you will no longer be free to sin!

The Lord Reveals His Trinitarian Life

And when Jesus was baptized, he went up immediately from the water, and behold, the heavens were opened and he saw the Spirit of God descending like a dove, and alighting on him; and lo, a voice from heaven, saying, "This is my beloved Son, with whom I am well pleased."

MATTHEW 3:16-17

MORNING READING

On the Tuesday following Ascension Thursday, having remained a while in prayer after Communion, I was grieved because I was so distracted I couldn't concentrate. So I complained to the Lord about our miserable nature. My soul began to enkindle, and it seemed to me I knew clearly in an intellectual vision that the entire Blessed Trinity was present. In this state my soul understood by a certain kind of representation (like an illustration of the truth), in such a way that my dullness could perceive, how God is three and one. And so it seemed that all three Persons were represented distinctly in my soul and that they spoke to me, telling me that from this day I would see an improvement in myself in respect to three things and that each one of these Persons would grant me a favor: one, the favor of charity; another, the favor of being able to suffer gladly; and the third, the favor of experiencing this charity with an enkindling in the soul.

Holy, holy, holy! Lord God Almighty!
Early in the morning our song shall rise to Thee;
Holy, holy, holy! Merciful and mighty!
God in three persons, blessed Trinity!

REGINALD HEBER, 1826

FOR REFLECTION

Lord, You are too great for us to ever fully understand. Each day may you favor me with a glimpse of how great You are, that I may never cease to praise You as I ought!

EVENING READING

[Editor's note: In this reading St. Teresa is referring to one of the blessings reserved for those drawn into the sixth chamber of the castle —imaginary visions seen by the "inner eye" of the soul.] The brilliance of this inner vision is like that of an infused light coming from a sun covered by something as transparent as a properly-cut diamond. Almost every time God grants this favor the soul is in rapture, for in its lowliness it cannot suffer so frightening a sight. I say "frightening" because although the Lord's presence is the most beautiful and delightful a person could imaging even were he to live and labor a thousand years thinking about it this presence bears such extraordinary majesty that it causes the soul extreme fright.

The one among you who feels safest should fear more, for blessed is the man who fears the Lord, says David. May His Majesty protect us always. To beseech Him that we not offend Him is the greatest security we can have. May He be praised forever, amen.

DAY 11
The Beauty of the Soul

Who shall ascend the hill of the Lord?
And who shall stand in his holy place?
He who has clean hands and a pure heart,
Who does not lift up his soul to what is false,
And does not swear deceitfully.
He will receive a blessing from the Lord,
And vindication from the God of his salvation.

PSALM 24:3-5

MORNING READING

The soul of the just person is nothing else but a paradise where the Lord says He finds His delight. His Majesty in saying that the soul is made in His own image makes it almost impossible for us to understand the sublime dignity and beauty of the soul. Because we have heard and because faith tells us so, we know we have souls. But we seldom consider the precious things that can be found in this soul, or who dwells within it, or its high value. Consequently, little effort is made to preserve its beauty. All our attention is taken up with the plainness of the diamond's setting or the outer wall of the castle; that is, with these bodies of ours.

What wondrous love is this, O my soul, O my soul?
What wondrous love is this, O my soul?
What wondrous love is this that caused the Lord of bliss
To bear the dreadful curse for my soul, for my soul;
To bear the dreadful curse for my soul?

ALEXANDER MEANS, 1801–1853

FOR REFLECTION

"The door of entry to this castle is prayer and reflection." Lord, give me the strength to journey tirelessly, the courage to continue faithfully, and the stillness to hear you quietly calling to me, guiding me on my way.

EVENING READING

If this castle is the soul, clearly one doesn't have to enter it since it is within oneself. But you must understand that there is a great difference in the ways one may be inside the castle. For there are many souls who are in the outer courtyard—which is where the guards stay—and don't care at all about entering the castle, nor do they know what lies within that most precious place, nor who is within, nor even how many rooms it has.

True, you will not be able to enter all the dwelling places through your own efforts, even though these efforts may seem to you great, unless the Lord of the castle Himself brings you there. Hence I advise you to use no force if you meet with any resistance, for you will thereby anger Him in such a way that He will never allow you to enter them. He is very fond of humility.

St. Martha: Our Role Model for Spiritual Service

Now as [Jesus] ... entered a village, a woman named Martha received him into her house. And she had a sister called Mary, who sat at the Lord's feet and listened to his teaching. But Martha was distracted with much serving; and she went to him and said, "Lord, do you not care that my sister has left me to serve alone? Tell her then to help me." But the Lord answered her, "Martha, Martha, you are anxious and troubled about many things; one thing is needful. Mary has chosen the good portion, which shall not be taken away from her."

LUKE 10:38-42

MORNING READING

Don't be afraid that you will fail to reach the perfection of those who are very contemplative. St. Martha was a saint, even though they do not say she was contemplative. Well now, what more do you want than to be able to resemble this blessed woman who merited so often to have Christ our Lord in her home, give Him food, serve Him, and eat at table with Him? If she had been enraptured like the Magdalene, there wouldn't have been anyone to give food to the divine Guest.

There must be people for every task. And those who are led by the active life shouldn't complain about those who are very much absorbed in contemplation, for these active ones know that the Lord will defend the contemplatives, even though these latter are silent since for the most part contemplation makes one forgetful of self and of all things. Let them consider how true humility consists very much in great readiness to be content with whatever the

Lord may want to do with them and in always finding oneself worthy to be called His servant.

All for Jesus! All for Jesus! All my being's ransomed pow'rs;
All my thoughts and words and doings,
*   all my days and all my hours.*
O, what wonder! How amazing! Jesus, glorious King of kings.
Deigns to call me His beloved, lets me rest beneath His wings.
                                                MARY D. JAMES, 1889

FOR REFLECTION
When I experience times of spiritual dryness and cannot feel your presence, Lord, give me strength to serve You faithfully.

EVENING READING
Let us desire and be occupied in prayer not for the sake of our enjoyment but so as to have this strength to serve. Let's refuse to take an unfamiliar path, for we shall get lost at the most opportune time. Believe me, Martha and Mary must join together in order to show hospitality to the Lord and have Him always present and not host Him badly by failing to give Him something to eat. How would Mary, always seated at His feet, provide Him with food if her sister did not help her? His food is that in every way possible we draw souls that they may be saved and praise Him always.

DAY 13
Persevering in Acts of Faith and Love

As an apple tree among the trees of the wood,
So is my beloved among young men.
With great delight I sat in his shadow,
And his fruit was sweet to my taste.
He brought me to his banqueting house,
And his banner over me was love.
Sustain me with raisins, refresh me with apples;
For I am sick with love.   SONG OF SOLOMON 2:3-5

MORNING READING

[Editor's note: The wording of the RSV differs slightly from the expression used by St. Teresa; the point is not lost, however—in fact, one would think she'd derive even greater refreshment from the raisins than the flowers (though they might not smell as sweet!)]
"Sustain me with flowers and surround me with apples, for I am dying of love." What flowers will these be? Flowers will provide no remedy unless you ask for them so as to die, for in truth nothing else is desired when the soul arrives here.

The fragrance of these flowers is different from the fragrance of flowers we smell here below. I understand by these words that the soul is asking to perform great works in the service of our Lord and of its neighbor. Although a person's life will become more active than contemplative, and one will seemingly lose if the petition is granted, Martha and Mary never fail to work almost together when the soul is in this state. For in the active—and seemingly exterior—work the soul is working interiorly. And when the active works rise from this interior root, they become lovely and very fragrant flowers. The fragrance from these flowers spreads to the benefit of many. It is a fragrance that lasts, not passing quickly, but having great effect.

From these flowers comes the fruit, the apples of which the bride then says: *Surround me with apples.* Give me trials, Lord; give me persecutions. And truly this soul desires them and indeed passes through them well. For since it no longer looks to its own satisfaction but to what pleases God, its pleasure is in somehow imitating the laborious life that Christ lived.

Spirit of God, descend upon my heart.
Wean it from earth, through all its pulses move;
Stoop to my weakness, mighty as Thou art,
And make me love Thee as I ought to love.

GEORGE CROLY, 1867

FOR REFLECTION
May the purity of my heart be revealed in my actions, and may everything I do expand my soul a little more to make room for You.

EVENING READING
May You be pleased, my God, that there come a time in which I may be able to repay You even one mite of all I owe You. Ordain, Lord, as You wish, how this servant of Yours may in some manner serve You. Fortify my soul and dispose it first, Good of all goods and my Jesus, and then ordain ways in which I might do something for You, for there is no longer anyone who can suffer to receive so much and not repay anything. Cost what it may, Lord, do not desire that I come into Your presence with hands so empty, since the reward must be given in conformity with one's deeds. Here is my life, here is my honor and my will. I have given all to You, I am Yours, make use of me according to Your will. I can do all things, provided You do not leave me.

Our Friendship With God Is Revealed by Our Actions

"Holy Father, keep them in thy name, which thou hast given me, that they may be one, even as we are one.... I have given them thy word; and the world has hated them because they are not of the world, even as I am not of the world. I do not pray that thou shouldst take them out of the world, but that thou shouldst keep them from the evil one. They are not of the world, even as I am not of the world. Sanctify them in the truth; thy word is truth."

JOHN 17:11b, 14-17

MORNING READING

When I began to take the first steps toward founding this monastery, it was not my intention that there be so much external austerity or that the house have no income; on the contrary, I would have desired the possibility that nothing be lacking. I realized I was a woman and wretched and incapable of doing any of the useful things I desired to do in the service of the Lord. All my longing was and still is that since He has so many enemies and so few friends that these few friends be good ones. As a result I resolved to do the little that was in my power; that is, to follow the evangelical counsels as perfectly as I could and strive that these few persons who live here do the same.

What is the matter with Christians nowadays? Must it always be those who owe You the most who afflict You?

All you who seek a comfort sure in sadness and distress,
Whatever sorrow burdens you, whatever griefs oppress;
When Jesus gave himself for us and died upon the tree,
His heart was pierced for love of us; he died to set us free.

EDWARD CASWELL, 1814–1878

FOR REFLECTION

Can I say I am a friend of God? What have I done today to strengthen that friendship?

EVENING READING

The Lord doesn't look so much at the greatness of our works as at the love with which they are done. And if we do what we can, His Majesty will enable us each day to do more and more, provided that we do not quickly tire. But during the little while this life lasts—and perhaps it will last a shorter time than each one thinks—let us offer the Lord interiorly and exteriorly the sacrifice we can. His Majesty will join it with that which He offered on the cross to the Father for us. Thus even though our works are small they will have the value our love for Him would have merited had they been great.

Take My Life and Let It Be ...

The Soul's Pursuit of Virtue

Keys to Lasting Peace:
Love, Detachment, and Humility

*Have no anxiety about anything, but in everything by prayer and
supplication with thanksgiving let your requests be made known to
God. And the peace of God, which passes all understanding, will
keep your hearts and your minds in Christ Jesus.*

PHILIPPIANS 4:6-8

MORNING READING

Do not think, my friends and daughters, that I shall burden you
with many things. I shall enlarge on only three things, for the
practice of these three things helps us to possess inwardly and
outwardly the peace our Lord recommended so highly to us. The
first of these is love for one another; the second is detachment
from all created things; the third is true humility, which, even
though I speak of it last, is the main practice and embraces all the
others.

> *Take my life and let it be*
> *Consecrated, Lord, to Thee;*
> *Take my hands and let them move*
> *At the impulse of Thy love...*

FRANCES R. HAVERGAL, 1874

FOR REFLECTION

"We must distinguish what is to be admired from what is to be imitated." Lord, help me to fulfill the job you have given me to do, and not to take on that which you have entrusted to another. May my life today be a unique expression of worship and bring honor to your holy name.

EVENING READING

When the Lord begins to give a virtue, it should be highly esteemed; and we should in no way place ourselves in the danger of losing it. Let any person who wants to advance and yet feels concerned about some point of honor believe me and strive to overcome this attachment, which is like a chain that cannot be broken by any file but only by God through our prayer and earnest cooperation. It seems to me that such attachment is a shackle on this road—I am astonished at the harm it does.

The devil sometimes makes the soul think it is obliged to receive honor. Well, let them believe me; if they don't remove this caterpillar, even though it doesn't damage the tree completely, since some other virtues will remain, all the virtues will be worm-eaten. The tree isn't a beautiful one, nor does it flourish, nor does it even allow the others that are near it to flourish. The fruit of good example that it gives is not healthy; it will last only a short while.

DAY 16
The Virtuous Soul

"Come, and I will show you the Bride, the wife of the Lamb." And in the Spirit he carried me away to a great, high mountain, and showed me the holy city Jerusalem coming down out of heaven from God, having the glory of God, its radiance like the most rare jewel, like a jasper, clear as crystal....

REVELATION 21:9b-11

MORNING READING

Let us imagine that within us is an extremely rich palace, built entirely of gold and precious stones. Imagine, too, that you have a part to play in order for the palace to be so beautiful; for there is no edifice as beautiful as is a soul pure and full of virtues. The greater the virtues, the more resplendent the jewels. Imagine, also, that in this palace dwells this mighty King who has been gracious enough to become your Father; and that He is seated upon an extremely valuable throne, which is your heart.

In my opinion, if I had understood as I do now that in this little palace of my soul dwelt so great a King, I would not have left Him alone so often. I would have remained with Him at times, and striven more so as not to be so unclean. But what a marvelous thing, that He who would fill a thousand worlds and many more with His grandeur would enclose Himself in something so small!

Finish then Thy new creation, pure and spotless let us be.
Let us see Thy great salvation perfectly restored in Thee.
Changed from glory into glory, till in heaven we take our place,
Till we cast our crowns before Thee,
   lost in wonder, love and praise!

CHARLES WESLEY, 1747

FOR REFLECTION

"We should walk in truth before God and people in as many ways as possible."

EVENING READING

Beginners must realize that in order to give delight to the Lord they are starting to cultivate a garden on very barren soil, full of abominable weeds. His Majesty pulls up the weeds and plants good seed. Now let us keep in mind that all of this is already done by the time a soul is determined to practice prayer and has begun to make use of it. And with the help of God we must strive like good gardeners to get these plants to grow and take pains to water them so that they don't wither but come to bud and flower and give forth a most pleasant fragrance to provide refreshment for this Lord of ours.

Practicing Forgiveness

For if you forgive men their trespasses,
your heavenly Father also will forgive you;
but if you do not forgive men their trespasses,
neither will your Father forgive your trespasses.

MATTHEW 6:14-15

MORNING READING

How the Lord must esteem this love we have for one another! Indeed, Jesus could have put other virtues first and said: forgive us, Lord, because we do a great deal of penance or because we pray much and fast or because we have left all for You and love You very much. He didn't say forgive us because we have given up our lives for You, or, as I say, because of other possible things. But He said only, "forgive us because we forgive." Perhaps he said the prayer and offered it on our behalf because He knows we are so fond of this miserable honor and that to be forgiving is a virtue difficult for us to attain by ourselves but most pleasing to His Father.

There's not a plant or flower below but makes Thy glories known;
And clouds arise, and tempests blow, by order from Thy throne;
While all that borrows life from Thee is ever in Thy care,
And everywhere that man may be, Thou God art present there.

ISAAC WATTS, 1674–1748

FOR REFLECTION

"Strive as much as you can, without offense to God, to be affable and understanding in such a way that everyone you talk to will love your conversation and desire your manner of living and acting, and not be frightened and intimidated by virtue."

EVENING READING

This is a matter that we should reflect upon very much: that something so serious and important, as that our Lord forgive us our faults, which deserve eternal fire, be done by means of something so lowly as our forgiving others. And I have so little opportunity to offer even this lowly thing, that the Lord has to pardon me for nothing. Here Your mercy fits in well. May you be blessed for putting up with one so poor as I.

Virtue by Association

Blessed is the man who walks not in the counsel of the wicked, nor stands in the way of sinners, nor sits in the seat of scoffers; but his delight is in the law of the Lord, and on his law he meditates day and night. He is like a tree planted by streams of water, that yields its fruit in its season, and its leaf does not wither. In all that he does, he prospers.

PSALM 1:1-3

MORNING READING

I had some first cousins who often came to our house, though my father was very cautious and would not allow others to do so; please God he had been inspired to do likewise with my cousins. For now I realize what a danger it is at an age when one should begin to cultivate the virtues to associate with people who do not know the vanity of the world but rather are just getting ready to throw themselves into it. I listened to accounts of their affections and of childish things not the least bit edifying; and, what was worse, I exposed my soul to that which caused all its harm.

From such experience I understand the great profit that comes from good companionship. If at that age I had gone around with virtuous persons, I would have remained whole in virtue. For should I have had when that age someone to teach me to fear God, my soul would have gained strength not to fall. Having lost this fear of God completely, I only had the fear of losing my reputation, and such fear brought me torment in everything I did. With the thought that my deeds would not be known, I dared to do many things truly against my honor and against God.

In shady, green pastures, so rich and so sweet,
God leads His dear children along;
Where water's cool flow bathes the weary one's feet,
God leads His dear children along.
Some thru the waters, some thru the flood,
Some thru the fire, but all thru the blood;
Some thru great sorrow, but God gives a song,
In the night season and all the day long.

G.A. YOUNG, 19TH CENTURY

FOR REFLECTION

"If I should have to give advice, I would tell parents that when their children are this age they ought to be very careful about whom their children associate with. For here lies the root of great evil since our natural bent is toward the worst rather than toward the best."

EVENING READING

We should take great care ... that our speech be edifying; we must flee those places where conversations are not of God. It's very necessary that this fear be deeply impressed within the soul. Such fear is easy to obtain if there is true love together with a great inner determination, as I have said, not to commit an offense against God or any created thing.

Often a servant of God, without uttering a word, prevents things from being said against God. This must happen for the same reason that something similar happens here below: there is always some restraint so as not to offend an absent person in the presence of someone known to be his friend. So it is with a servant of God: his friendship with God wins him respect no matter how lowly his status, and others avoid afflicting him in a matter they so well realize would grieve him; that is, they avoid offending God in his presence.

DAY 19
Growth in Virtue Requires Diligence

Therefore, beloved, since you wait for these, be zealous to be found by him without spot or blemish, and at peace. And count the forbearance of our Lord as salvation.

2 PETER 3:14-15a

MORNING READING

We must always ask God in prayer to sustain us, and very often think that if He abandons us we will soon end in the abyss; and we must never trust in ourselves since it would be foolish to do so. Then, we should walk with special care and attention, observing how we are proceeding in the practice of virtue: whether we are getting better or worse in some areas, especially in love for one another. His Majesty would regret the loss of a soul so much that He gives it in many ways a thousand interior warnings, so that the harm will not be hidden from it.

Let this, in sum, be the conclusion: that we strive always to advance. And if we don't advance, let us walk with great fear. Love is never idle, and a failure to grow would be a very bad sign. A soul that has tried to be the betrothed of God Himself, that is not intimate with His Majesty, and has reached the boundaries that were mentioned, must not go to sleep.

There is a place of quiet rest, near to the heart of God,
A place where sin cannot molest, near to the heart of God.
O Jesus, blest Redeemer, sent from the heart of God
Hold us who wait before Thee near to the heart of God.

CLELAND B. MCAFEE, 1866–1944

FOR REFLECTION

"If we fail in love of neighbor we are lost."

EVENING READING

Let's not think that everything is accomplished through much weeping but set our hands to the task of hard work and virtue. These are what we must pay attention to; let the tears come when God sends them and without any effort on our part to induce them. These tears from God will irrigate this dry earth, and they are a great help in producing fruit. The less attention we pay to them the more there are, for they are the water that falls from heaven. The tears we draw out by tiring ourselves in digging cannot compare with the tears that come from God, for often in digging we shall get worn out and not find even a puddle of water much less a flowing well. Therefore, I consider it better for us to place ourselves in the presence of the Lord and look at His mercy and grandeur and at our own lowliness, and let Him give us what He wants, whether water or dryness. He knows best what is suitable for us.

The Virtuous Soul Is Like a Garden

*If you pour yourself out for the hungry and satisfy the desire of the
afflicted, then shall your light rise in the darkness and your gloom
be as the noonday. And the Lord will guide you continually, and
satisfy your desire with good things ... and you shall be like a
watered garden, like a spring of water whose waters fail not.*

ISAIAH 58:10-11

MORNING READING

It was a great delight for me to consider my soul as a garden and
reflect that the Lord was taking His walk in it. I begged Him to
increase the fragrance of the little flowers of virtue that were
beginning to blossom, so it seemed, and that they might give Him
glory and He might sustain them since I desired nothing for
myself—and that He might cut the ones He wanted, for I already
knew that better ones would flower.

Everything seems to be dry, and it seems there is not going to
be any water to sustain it—nor does it appear that there has ever
been in the soul anything of virtue. It undergoes much tribulation
because the Lord desires that it seem to the poor gardener that
everything acquired in watering and keeping the garden up is
being lost.

It seems to me the garden can be watered in four ways. You
may draw water from a well (which is for us a lot of work). Or you
may get it by means of a water wheel and aqueducts in such a way
that it is obtained by turning the crank of the water wheel (I have
drawn it this way sometimes—the method involves less work than
the other, and you get more water). It may flow from a river or a
stream (the garden is watered much better by this means because
the ground is more fully soaked, and there is no need to water so
frequently—and much less work for the gardener). Or the water

may be provided by a great deal of rain (for the Lord waters the garden without any work on our part—and this way is incomparably better than all the others mentioned).

> *There is a fountain filled with blood drawn from Immanuel's*
> *veins,*
> *And sinners plunged beneath that flood lose all their guilty stains.*
> *Lose all their guilty stains, lose all their guilty stains;*
> *And sinners plunged beneath that flood lose all their guilty stains.*
>
> WILLIAM COWPER, 1731–1800

FOR REFLECTION

When you walk in the garden of my soul, Lord, what do you see—weeds and brambles? Or a well-tended plot?

EVENING READING

[Editor's note: In this reading St. Teresa makes reference to the fifth room of the castle. Although the saint assures us that "very few" fail to enter, the fifth room of the castle is inhabited by those who have experienced profound spiritual graces and are well on the way to attaining spiritual union, as illustrated from the butterfly breaking from the cocoon.] There are indeed only a few who fail to enter this dwelling place of which I shall now speak. There are various degrees, and for that reason I say that most enter these places. But I believe that only a few will experience some of the things that I will say are in this room. Yet even if souls do no more than reach the door, God is being very merciful to them; although many are called few are chosen (Mt 22:14).

So, since in some way we can enjoy heaven on earth, be brave in begging the Lord to give us His grace in such a way that nothing will be lacking through our own fault; that He show us the way and strengthen the soul that it may dig until it finds this hidden treasure. The truth is that the treasure lies within our very selves.

I Need Thee Every Hour ...

*The Soul's Quest for Humility
and Self-Knowledge*

DAY 21
The Importance of Self-Knowledge

"God opposes the proud, but gives grace to the humble." Submit yourselves therefore to God. Resist the devil and he will flee from you. Draw near to God and he will draw near to you. Cleanse your hands, you sinners, and purify your hearts, you men of double mind. Be wretched and mourn and weep. Let your laughter be turned to mourning and your joy to dejection. Humble yourselves before God and he will exalt you."

JAMES 4:6b-10

MORNING READING

[Editor's note: In this reading, St. Teresa refers to the first room of the soul's castle, which contains many smaller chambers that must be explored before pressing toward the center. A spiritual "boot camp," so to speak.] It is very important for any soul that practices prayer, whether little or much, not to hold itself back and stay in one corner [of the castle]. Let it walk through these dwelling places which are up above, down below, and to the sides, since God has given it such great dignity. Don't force it to stay a long time in one room alone. Oh, but if it is in the room of self-knowledge! How necessary this room is even for those whom the Lord has brought into the very dwelling place where He abides.

Humility, like the bee making honey in the beehive, is always at work. Without it, everything goes wrong. But let's remember that the bee doesn't fail to leave the beehive and fly about gathering nectar from the flowers. So it is with the soul in the room of self-knowledge; let it believe me and fly sometimes to ponder the grandeur and majesty of its God. Here it will discover its lowliness better than by thinking of itself, and be freer from the vermin that enter the first rooms, those of self-knowledge.

I need Thee every hour, most gracious Lord;
No tender voice like Thine can peace afford.
I need Thee, O I need Thee; every hour I need Thee;
O bless me now, my Savior, I come to Thee.

ANNIE S. HAWKS, 1872

FOR REFLECTION

Help me, Lord, not to care as much about how others see me as how You see me. Grant me the grace I need to change those areas that do not please You.

EVENING READING

O Lord, take into account the many things we suffer on this path for lack of knowledge! Terrible trials are suffered because we don't understand ourselves, and that which isn't bad at all but good we think is a serious fault. Just as we cannot stop the movement of the heavens, so neither can we stop our mind; and then the faculties of the soul go with it, and we think we are lost and have wasted the time spent before God. But the soul is perhaps completely joined with Him in the dwelling places very close to the center while the mind is on the outskirts of the castle suffering from a thousand wild and poisonous beasts, and meriting by this suffering. As a result we should not be disturbed; nor should we abandon prayer, which is what the devil wants us to do. For the most part all the trials and disturbances come from our not understanding ourselves.

DAY 22
Guarding Against False Humility

*Do nothing from selfishness or conceit, but in humility count
others better than yourselves. Let each of you look not only to his
own interests, but also to the interests of others. Have this mind
among yourselves, which was in Christ Jesus, who, though he was
in the form of God, did not count equality with God a thing to be
grasped, but emptied himself, taking the form of a servant, being
born in the likeness of men.... Work out your own salvation with
fear and trembling; for God is at work in you, both to will and to
work for his good pleasure.*

PHILIPPIANS 2:3-7, 12-13

MORNING READING

I shall tell you about one lady in particular. She was very fond of
receiving Communion frequently, never said anything bad about
anyone, experienced devotion in her prayer, and lived in constant
solitude because she was in her house by herself. She was so mild
in her temperament that nothing said to her ever made her angry
or say any bad word, for she was quite perfect. Since I saw all these
virtues, it seemed to me they were effects of a very advanced soul
and of deep prayer.

After getting to know her I began to understand that all was
peaceful as long as her self-interest was not affected. Although she
would suffer all the things that were said against her, she would
not tolerate anything said against her reputation even in some tiny
point concerning her honor or the esteem she thought was her
due.

I did not envy her manner of living and sanctity. Rather, she
and two other souls that I have seen in this life who were saints in

their own opinion, caused me more fear, after I spoke with them, than all the sinners I have seen. I beg the Lord to give us light.

Amazing grace! How sweet the sound, that saved a wretch like me!
I once was lost, but now am found, was blind, but now I see.
JOHN NEWTON, 1725–1807

FOR REFLECTION

"People living in their own homes cannot know their faults, even though they would like to because they want to please the Lord. For, in the end, what they do is their own will." Lord, even when no one else is around, You are there. Help me to be aware of the areas of my life that do not please You.

EVENING READING

With regard to the fear about whether or not I was in the state of grace, He told me: "Daughter, light is very different from darkness. I am faithful. Nobody will be lost unknowingly. They who find security in spiritual favors will be deceived. True security is the testimony of a good conscience. But people should not think that through their own efforts they can be in light or that they can do anything to prevent the night, because these states depend upon my grace. The best help for holding on to the light is to understand that you can do nothing and that it comes from me. For even though you may be in light, at the moment I withdraw, the night will come. This is true humility: to know what you can do and what I can do."

Guarding Against Spiritual Pride

"Two men went up to the temple to pray, one a Pharisee and the other a tax collector. The Pharisee stood and prayed thus with himself, 'God, I thank thee I am not like other men, extortioners, unjust, adulterers, or even like this tax collector....' But the tax collector, standing far off, would not even lift his eyes to heaven, but beat his breast, saying, 'God, be merciful to me a sinner!' I tell you, this man went down to his house justified rather than the other; for every one who exalts himself will be humbled, but he who humbles himself will be exalted."

LUKE 18:10-14

MORNING READING

The devil sets up another dangerous temptation: self-assurance in the thought that we will in no way return to our past faults and worldly pleasures: "for now I have understood the world and know that all things come to an end and that the things of God give me greater delight." If this self-assurance is present in beginners, it is very dangerous because with it a person doesn't take care against entering once more into the occasions of sin, and he falls flat; please God the relapse will not bring about something much worse. For since the devil sees that he is dealing with a soul that can do him harm and bring profit to others, he uses all his power so that it might not rise.

Depth of mercy! Can there be mercy still reserved for me?
Can my God His wrath forbear? Me, the chief of sinners spare?
I have long withstood his grace, long provoked Him to His face,
Would not hearken to His calls, grieved Him by a thousand falls.
Still for me my Savior stands, holding forth His wounded hands;
God is love! I know, I feel; Jesus weeps and loves me still.

CHARLES WESLEY, 1740

FOR REFLECTION

"However sublime the contemplation, let your prayer always begin and end with self-knowledge."

EVENING READING

I wouldn't consider it safe for a soul, however favored by God, to forget that at one time it saw itself in a miserable state. Although recalling this misery is a painful thing, doing so is helpful for many.

No relief is afforded this suffering by the thought that our Lord has already pardoned and forgotten the sins. Rather, it adds to the suffering to see so much goodness and realize that favors are granted to one who deserves nothing but hell. I think such a realization was the great martyrdom for St. Peter and the Magdalene. Since their love for God had grown so deep and they had received so many favors and come to know the grandeur and majesty of God, the remembrance of their misery would have been difficult to suffer, and they would have suffered it with tender sentiments.

DAY 24
The Dangers of Intellectual Pride

If I speak in the tongues of men and of angels, but have not love, I am a noisy gong or a clanging cymbal. And if I have prophetic powers, and understand all mysteries and all knowledge ... but have not love, I am nothing.... Love never ends; as for prophesies, they will pass away; as for tongues, they will cease; as for knowledge, it will pass away. For our knowledge is imperfect; but when the perfect comes, the imperfect will pass away.

1 CORINTHIANS 13:1-2, 8-10

MORNING READING

Some learned men (whom the Lord does not lead by this mode of [contemplative] prayer and who haven't begun a life of prayer) want to be so rational about things and so precise in their understanding that it doesn't seem anyone else but they with their learning can understand the grandeurs of God. If only they could learn something from the humility of the most Blessed Virgin!

As to what you say about those who parade their learning, it would be extremely unfortunate if that defect were found in (people who really have) so little (to parade). If a person shows signs of that so quickly it would be better for him not to have any learning at all.

Let all mortal flesh keep silence, and with fear and trembling
*   stand;*
Ponder nothing earthly minded, for with blessing in His hand,
Christ our God to earth descendeth, our full homage to demand.
At his feet the six-winged Seraph, Cherumbim, with sleepless eye,
Veil their faces to the presence, as with ceaseless voice they cry,
Alleluia, Alleluia, Alleluia, Lord most high!

LITURGY OF ST. JAMES, 5TH CENTURY
ADAPTED BY GERARD MOULTRIE, 1864

FOR REFLECTION

Lord, give me an opportunity today to practice humility—even if it means appearing foolish in someone else's eyes!

EVENING READING

Humility does not disturb or disquiet or agitate, however great it may be; it comes with peace, delight, and calm. Even though a person upon seeming himself so wretched understands clearly that he merits to be in hell, suffers affliction, thinks everyone should in justice abhor him, and almost doesn't dare to ask for mercy, his pain, if the humility is genuine, comes with a sweetness in itself and a satisfaction that he wouldn't want to be without. *The pain of genuine humility doesn't agitate or afflict the soul; rather, this humility expands it and enables it to serve God more.*

The Benefit of Knowing Oneself

O Lord, thou has searched me and known me! Thou knowest when I sit down and when I rise up; thou discernest my thoughts from afar…. Such knowledge is too wonderful for me; it is high, I cannot attain it.

PSALM 139:1-2, 6

MORNING READING

The soul is like water in a glass: the water looks very clear if the sun doesn't shine on it; but when the sun shines on it, it seems to be full of dust particles. This comparison is an exact one. Before being in this ecstasy the soul thinks it is careful about not offending God and that it is doing what it can in conformity with its strength. But once it is brought into prayer, which this Sun of justice bestows on it and which opens its eyes, it sees so many dust particles that it would want to close its eyes again. It is not yet so much a child of this powerful eagle that it can gaze steadily at this sun. But for the little time that it holds its eyes open, it sees that it is itself filled with mud. It recalls the psalm that says *Who will be just in Your Presence?* [See Psalm 143:2.]

When it beholds this divine Sun, the brightness dazzles it; when it looks at itself, the mud covers its eyes; blind is this little dove. So, very frequently, it is left totally blind, absorbed, frightened, and in a swoon from the many grandeurs that it sees. In this stage true humility is gained so that the soul doesn't care at all about saying good things of itself, nor that others say them. The Lord, not the soul, distributes the fruit of the garden, and so nothing sticks to its hands. All the good it possesses is directed to God.

Just as I am, without one plea but that Thy blood was shed for me,
And that Thou bidd'st me come to Thee,
    O Lamb of God, I come! I come!
Just as I am, poor, wretched, blind—sight, riches, healing of the
    mind,
Yea, all I need in Thee I find—O Lamb of God, I come! I come!
                              CHARLOTTE ELLIOTT, 1789–1871

FOR REFLECTION

"May You be blessed, my Lord, that from such filthy mud as I, You make water so clear that it can be served at Your table! May You be praised, O Joy of the angels, for having desired to raise up a worm so vile!"

EVENING READING

Knowledge of the grandeur of God, self-knowledge and humility upon seeing something so low in comparison with the Creator, little esteem of earthly things save for those that can be used in the service of so great a God: These are the jewels the Spouse begins to give the betrothed, and their value is such that the soul will not want to lose them. For these meetings remain so engraved in the memory that I believe it's impossible to forget them until one enjoys them forever, unless they are forgotten through one's own most serious fault. But the Spouse who gives them has the power to give the grace not to lose them.

Back to Basics:
Guarding Against Our Own Faults

*Judge not, that you be not judged. For with the judgment you
pronounce you will be judged, and the measure you give will be
the measure you get. Why do you see the speck that is in your
brother's eye, but do not notice the log that is in your own eye?...
First take the log out of your own eye, then you will see clearly to
take the speck out of your brother's eye.*

MATTHEW 7:1-3, 5

MORNING READING

There is no stage of prayer so sublime that it isn't necessary to
return often to the beginning. Along this path of prayer, self-
knowledge and the thought of one's sins is the bread with which
all palates must be fed no matter how delicate they may be; they
cannot be sustained without this bread. It must be eaten within
bounds, nonetheless. Once a soul sees that it is now submissive
and understands clearly that it has nothing good of itself and is
aware both of being ashamed before so great a King and of
repaying so little of the great amount it owes Him—what need is
there to waste time here? We must go on to other things that the
Lord places before us; and there is no reason to leave them aside,
for His Majesty knows better than we what is fitting for us to eat.

Frail children of dust, and feeble as frail,
In Thee do we trust, nor find Thee to fail;
Thy mercies how tender! how firm to the end!
Our Maker, Defender, Redeemer and Friend.

WILLIAM KETHE, 1561
ADAPT. BY ROBERT GRANT, 1833

FOR REFLECTION

"It is a great mistake to think you know everything, and then say you are humble."

EVENING READING

Always grieve over any fault, if it is publicly known, that you see in a Sister. Here love shows itself, and is practiced well when you know how to suffer the fault and not be surprised.

Recommend the Sister to God, and strive yourself to practice with great perfection the virtue opposite the fault that appears in her. Make every effort to do this so that you teach that Sister in deed what perhaps through words or punishment she might not understand or profit by; and the imitation of the virtue in which one sees another excel has a great tendency to spread.

Showers of Blessing ...

The Soul's Thirst for Courage

DAY 27
Water for the Thirsty Soul

As a hart longs for flowing streams,
so longs my soul for thee, O God.
My soul thirsts for God, for the living God.
When shall I come and behold the face of my God?

PSALM 42:1-2

MORNING READING

The Savior said to the Samaritan woman, "whoever drinks of it will never thirst." How right and true, as words coming from the mouth of Truth Itself, that such a person will not thirst for anything in this life—although thirst for the things of the next life increases much more than can ever be imagined through natural thirst! When God satisfies the thirst, the greatest favor He can grant the soul is to leave it in the same need—and a greater one—to drink the water again.

Why do you think that I have tried to explain the goal and show you the reward before the battle, by telling you about the good that comes from drinking of this heavenly fount, of this living water? So that you will not be dismayed by the trial and contradiction there is along the way, and advance with courage and not grow weary. It can happen that after having arrived you will have nothing left to do but stoop and drink from the fount; and yet you will abandon everything and lose this good, thinking that you have not the strength to reach it and that you are not meant for it.

Behold, the Lord invites us all. He could have said, "Come all of you, for in the end you won't lose anything, and to those whom I choose I will give to drink." But since He spoke without this condition to all, I hold as certain that all those who do not falter on the way will drink this living water.

"There shall be showers of blessing" —*O that today they might fall,*
Now as to God we're confessing, now as on Jesus we call!
Showers of blessing, Showers of blessing we need;
Mercy-drops round us are falling, But for the showers we plead.
DANIEL W. WHITTLE, 1840–1901

FOR REFLECTION
When I am feeling drained from life, Lord, teach me to return again and again to the waters of your grace, which never run dry!

EVENING READING
Rivers stream from this overflowing fount, some large, others small; and sometimes little pools for children—for that is enough for them, and moreover it would frighten them at the beginning. So, do not fear that you will die of thirst on this road. Never is the lack of consoling water such that it cannot be endured. Since this is so, take my advice and do not stop on the road but, like the strong, fight even to death in the search, for you are not here for any other reason than to fight.

Do not be frightened by the many things you need to consider in order to begin this divine journey which is the royal road to heaven. A great treasure is gained by traveling this road; no wonder we have to pay what seems to us a high price. The time will come when you will understand how trifling everything is next to so precious a reward.

Water: Refreshment and Cleansing

Behold, thou desirest truth in the inward being;
Therefore teach me wisdom in my secret heart.
Purge me with hyssop, and I shall be clean;
Wash me, and I shall be whiter than snow.

PSALM 51:6-7

MORNING READING

Water has three properties that I now recall as applicable to our subject. The first is that it refreshes; for, no matter how much heat we may experience, as soon as we approach the water the heat goes away.

Another property of water is that it cleans dirty things. Do you know how clean this water is when it isn't cloudy, when it isn't muddy, but falls from heaven? Once this water has been drunk, I am certain that it leaves the soul bright and cleansed of all faults.

The other property of water is that it satisfies to the full and takes away thirst. To me it seems that thirst signifies the desire for something of which we are in great want, so that if the thing is completely lacking its absence will kill us.

It should be understood that since there can be nothing imperfect in our supreme Good, everything He gives is for our good; and however great the abundance of this water He gives, there cannot be too much in anything of His. If He gives a great deal, He gives the soul, as I said, the capacity to drink much; like a glassmaker who makes the vessel a size he sees is necessary in order to hold what he intends to pour into it.

The King of love my Shepherd is, whose goodness faileth never;
I nothing lack if I am His, and He is mine forever.
Where streams of living water flow, my ransomed soul He leadeth,
And where the verdant pastures grow, with food celestial feedeth.

FROM PSALM 23

HENRY W. BAKER, 1821–1877

FOR REFLECTION

Holy Spirit, continue the work you began on the day of my baptism. Show me one parched, dry spot in my life today that you would like to restore to life.

EVENING READING

Just as all the streams that flow from a crystal-clear fount are also clear, the works of a soul in grace, because they proceed from this fount of life, in which the soul is planted like a tree, are most pleasing in the eyes of both God and man. It should be kept in mind that the fount, the shining sun that is in the center of the soul, does not lose its beauty and splendor; it is always present in the soul, and nothing can take away its loveliness. But if a black cloth is placed over a crystal that is in the sun, obviously the sun's brilliance will have no effect on the crystal even though the sun is shining on it.

Avoid Worldly "Peace"

Cast all your anxieties on him, for he cares about you. Be sober, be watchful. Your adversary the devil prowls around like a roaring lion, seeking some one to devour.

1 PETER 5:7-8

MORNING READING

God deliver you from the peace of many kinds that worldly people have. When such persons of the world remain quiet, while going about in serious sin, and so tranquil about their vices, for their consciences don't feel remorseful about anything, their peace is a sign that they and the devil are friends. For while they live, the devil does not wage war against them.

When a sister begins to grow lax in things that in themselves seem small, persisting in them for a long time without feeling any remorse of conscience, the resulting peace is bad. And consequently the devil can draw her into a thousand evils.

Yet she on earth hath union with God the Three in One,
And mystic sweet communion with those whose rest is won:
O happy ones and holy! Lord, give us grace that we,
Like them, the meek and lowly, on high may dwell with Thee.

SAMUEL J. STONE, 1839–1900

FOR REFLECTION

"For love of God be very careful. There must be war in this life."

EVENING READING

When you leave prayer you will meet a thousand little obstacles, a thousand little occasions to break one rule carelessly, or not to carry out another well, interior disturbances and temptations. It is a wonderful favor from the Lord. By this means the soul advances. It's impossible for us to be angels here below because such is not our nature. If love and fear of our Lord are present, the soul will gain very much; I'm certain of that. If I see a soul always quiet and without any war—for I've run into something like this—I always fear even if I do not see it offending the Lord.

O Holy Bride, let us turn to what you ask for: that holy peace which makes the soul, while remaining itself completely secure and tranquil, venture out to war against all worldly kinds of peace. Oh, how happy will be the lot of one who obtains this favor since it is union with the will of God; such a union that there is no division between Him and the soul, but one same will. It is a union not based on words or desires alone, but a union proved by deeds.

Courage to Pursue God

He who does not take his cross and follow me is not worthy of me.
He who finds his life will lose it, and he who loses his life for my
sake will find it.

MATTHEW 10:38-39

MORNING READING

I see clearly the great mercy the Lord bestowed on me; for though I continued to associate with the world, I had the courage to practice prayer. I say courage, for I do not know what would require greater courage among all the things there are in the world than to betray the king and know that he knows it and yet never leave His presence. Though we are always in the presence of God, it seems to me the manner is different with those who practice prayer, for they are aware that He is looking at them. With others, it can happen that several days pass without their recalling that God sees them.

From prayer that asks that I may be
Sheltered from winds that beat on Thee,
From fearing when I should aspire,
From faltering when I should climb higher.
From silken self, O Captain, free
Thy soldier who would follow Thee.

From subtle love of softening things
From easy choices, weakenings
Not thus are spirits fortified

Not this way went Thy Crucified
From all that dims Thy Calvary
O Lamb of God, deliver me !

Give me the love that leads the way,
The faith that nothing can dismay,
The hope no disappointment tires,
The passion that will burn like fire.
Let me not sink to be a clod.
Make me Thy fuel, O Flame of God.

AMY CARMICHAEL, 1867–1951

FOR REFLECTION

Courage, Lord—to see the enemy without as well as the enemy within.

EVENING READING

God does not deny Himself to anyone who perseveres. Little by little He will measure out the courage sufficient to attain this victory. I say "courage" because there are so many times the devil puts in the minds of beginners to prevent them in fact from starting out on this path. For he knows the damage that will be done to him in losing not only that one soul but many others.

God Patiently Waits for Us to Turn to Him

Seek the Lord while he may be found, call upon him
  while he is near;
Let the wicked forsake his way, and the unrighteous man
  his thoughts;
Let him return to the Lord, that he might have mercy on him,
And to our God, for he will abundantly pardon.

ISAIAH 55:6-7

MORNING READING

[Editor's note: The following passage refers to the second room of the castle. Those who have reached this room have relinquished many of their worldly attachments, and yet this process is not yet complete. In the second room, a few persistent "devils" try to lure the soul back to its previous fleshly way of life. The soul detaches itself from these snares by learning to love God more perfectly, and by attaining an even higher level of virtue and humility.] His Majesty knows well how to wait many days and years, especially when He sees perseverance and good desires. This perseverance is most necessary here. One always gains much through perseverance. But the attacks made by devils in a thousand ways afflict the soul more in these rooms than in the previous ones. In the previous ones the soul was deaf and dumb—at least it heard very little and resisted less, as one who has partly lost hope of conquering.

O Jesus, what an uproar the devils instigate here! And the afflictions of the poor soul: it doesn't know whether to continue or to return to the first room. Reason, for its part, shows the soul that it is mistaken in thinking that these things of the world are not worth anything when compared to what it is aiming after. Faith, however, teaches it about where it will find fulfillment.

> *Teach me to love Thee as Thine angels love,*
> *One holy passion filling all my frame;*
> *The baptism of the heav'n descended Dove,*
> *My heart an altar, and Thy love the flame.*

GEORGE CROLY, 1867

FOR REFLECTION

"Oh, how everything that is suffered with love is healed again!"

EVENING READING

There's no queen like humility for making the King surrender. *Humility drew the King from heaven to the womb of the Virgin, and with it, by one hair, we will draw Him to our souls.* And realize that the one who has more humility will be the one who possesses Him more; and the one who has less will possess Him less. For I cannot understand how there could be humility without love, or love without humility; nor are these two virtues possible without detachment from all creatures. The King of glory will not come to our soul—I mean to be united with it—if we do not make the effort to gain great virtues.

Heavenly Rain:
The Effortless Mystery of Contemplation

For land which has drunk the rain that often falls upon it, and brings forth vegetation useful to those for whose sake it is cultivated, receives a blessing from God....

HEBREWS 6:7

MORNING READING

Let us speak of this heavenly water that in its abundance soaks and saturates this entire garden: if the Lord were always to give it when there is need, the gardener would evidently have it easy. And if there were no winter and the weather were always mild, there would be no lack of flowers and fruit. It is obvious how delighted the gardener would be. But this is impossible while we are living on this earth. Individuals must always take care so that when one kind of water is lacking they must strive for another. This water from heaven often comes when the gardener is least expecting it. True, in the beginning it almost always occurs after a long period of mental prayer.

The Lord comes to take this tiny bird from one degree to another and to place it in the nest so that it may have repose. Since He has seen it fly about for a long time, striving with the intellect and the will and all its strength to see God and please Him, He desires to reward it even in this life. And what a tremendous reward; one moment is enough to repay all the trials that can be suffered in life!

I am not skilled to understand what God hath willed,
*   what God hath planned*
I only know at His right hand is One who is my Savior!
Yea, living, dying, let me bring my strength,
*   my solace from this spring*
That He who lives to be my King once died to be my Savior

DORA GREENWELL, 1821–1882

FOR REFLECTION

"In the spiritual world there are different kinds of weather; that is quite unavoidable. So do not be troubled by it, for it is no fault of yours."

EVENING READING

Oh, what a good time this is for you to harvest the fruits of the resolutions you have made to serve Our Lord! Remember, it is often His pleasure to test our actions and see if they match our resolutions and our words.

If you help yourselves, the good Jesus will help you; for, though He is asleep on the sea, when the storm rises He will still the winds. His pleasure is that we should ask Him for what we need, and so much does He love us that He is always seeking ways to help us. Blessed be His name for ever. Amen, amen, amen.

Be Thou My Vision ...

*Detaching the Soul From
Earthly Entanglements*

DAY 33

Detachment From Material Goods

A man named Ananias with his wife Sapphira sold a piece of property, and with his wife's knowledge he kept back some of the proceeds, and brought only a part and laid it at the apostles' feet. But Peter said, "Ananias, why has Satan filled your heart to lie to the Holy Spirit…? You have not lied to men but to God."

When Ananias heard these words, he fell down and died.

ACTS 5:1-3, 4b

MORNING READING

[Editor's note: The following passage was written to sisters who had taken a vow of poverty, and yet the message of stewardship is one we can all take to heart.] If people have easily what they need and a lot of money in their coffers and guard against committing serious sins, they think everything is done. They enjoy what they have. They give an alms from time to time. They do not reflect that their riches are not their own but given by the Lord so that they, as His stewards, may share their wealth among the poor, and that they must give a strict account for the time they keep a surplus in their coffers while delaying and putting off the poor who are suffering. Praise His Majesty because He has made you poor, and that you accept poverty as a particular favor from Him.

We must be content with little. We must not want as much as those who give a strict accounting, as any rich person will have to give, even though he may not have to do so here on earth. As for you, daughters, look always for the poorest things, which will be enough to get by on; in clothing as well as food. If you don't, you will find yourselves frustrated because God is not going to give you more, and you will be unhappy. Strive always to serve His

Majesty in such a way that you do not eat the food of the poor without serving Him for it.

> *Riches I heed not, nor man's empty praise—*
> *Thou mine inheritance, now and always;*
> *Thou and Thou only, first in my heart—*
> *High King of heaven, my treasure Thou art.*

IRISH HYMN, 8TH CENTURY
TRANSLATED BY MARY E. BYRNE, 1880–1931

FOR REFLECTION

"Honor and money almost always go together; anyone who wants honor doesn't despise money, and anyone who despises money doesn't care much about honor."

EVENING READING

Don't think, my Sisters, that because you do not strive to please those who are in the world you will lack food. I assure you that such will not be the case. Never seek sustenance through human schemes, for you will die of hunger—and rightly so. Your eyes on your Spouse! He will sustain you. Once He is pleased, those least devoted to you will give you food even though they may not want to, as you have seen through experience.

Our greatest gain is to lose the wealth which is of such a brief duration, and, by comparison with eternal things, of such little worth; yet we are upset about it and our gain turns into loss. But we must remember it is no consolation to say this to anyone whom God has not granted this favor [of complete detachment]: the only way to help such a one is to show him that we feel for his sorrow.

DAY 34
Detachment From Friends and Family

While he was still speaking to the people, behold, his mother and his brethren stood outside, asking to speak to him. But he replied to the man who told him, "Who is my mother, and who are my brethren?" And stretching out his hand toward his disciples, he said, "Here are my mother and my brethren! For whoever does the will of my Father in heaven is my brother, and sister, and mother."

MATTHEW 12:46-50

MORNING READING

[Editor's note: Again, this passage was written primarily for those who have chosen a religious calling. And yet, it also reminds us not to place the opinion of anyone—even family—higher than the call of one's own conscience.] I don't know what it is in the world that we renounce when we say that we give up everything for God if we do not give up the main thing, namely, our relatives. The situation has reached the state in which it seems to be a lack of virtue for religious not to love and talk a great deal with their relatives, and these religious are not afraid to say and even advance their reasons. In this house, daughters, great care should be taken to recommend them to God; that is right. As for the rest, we should keep them out of our minds as much as possible, because it is a natural thing for the will to become attached to them more than to other persons. Believe, Sisters, that if you serve His Majesty as you ought, you will not find better relatives than those He sends you.

That word above all earthly powers, No thanks to them, abideth;
The Spirit and the gifts are ours Through him who with us sideth:
Let goods and kindred go, This mortal life also:
  The body they may kill:
  God's truth abideth still;
His kingdom is forever.

MARTIN LUTHER, 1529
TRANSLATED BY FREDERICK H. HEDGE, 1852

FOR REFLECTION

Lord, thank you for my family. May the way I relate to each member be pleasing to you, and never bring you grief.

EVENING READING

[Editor's note: St. Teresa wrote this letter to her cousin, Don Diego de Guzman, upon hearing of his wife's death.] May the grace of the Holy Spirit be with you and give you the comfort you need in so great a loss as this seems to us now. But the Lord, Whose doing it is, and Who loves us more than we love ourselves, will show us in His own time that it was the greatest blessing that He could have bestowed upon my cousin and all those who wish her well; for He always takes souls when it is best for them.

You must not think of life as very long, for anything is short that comes to an end so quickly. Reflect that it is only into God's hands, for His Majesty will do what is best. It is the greatest comfort to witness a death which affords us the complete certainty that the departed one will live for ever. And you must believe that, if the Lord has taken her, she will help you and your daughters all the better now that she is in the presence of God.

Detachment From Injustice

If the world hates you, know that it has hated me before it hated you. If you were of the world, the world would love its own; but because you are not of the world, but I chose you out of the world, therefore the world hates you. Remember the word that I said to you, 'A servant is not greater than his master.' If they persecuted me, they will persecute you....

JOHN 15:18-20

MORNING READING

Run a thousand miles from such expressions as: "I was right." "They had no reason for doing this to me." "The one who did this to me was wrong." God deliver us from this poor way of reasoning. Does it seem to have been right that our good Jesus suffered so many insults and was made to undergo so much injustice? Either we are brides of so great a King or we are not. If we are, what honorable woman is there who does not share in the dishonors done to her spouse even though she does not will them? In fact, both spouses share the honor and the dishonor. Now, then, to enjoy a part in His kingdom and want no part in His dishonors and trials is nonsense.

O my Lord, when I think of the many ways You suffered and how You deserved none of these sufferings, I don't know what to say about myself, nor do I know where my common sense was when I didn't want to suffer, nor where I am when I excuse myself. You already know, my Good, that if I have some good it is a gift from no one else's hands but Yours. Don't allow, don't allow, my God—nor would I ever want You to allow—that there be anything in Your servant that is displeasing in Your eyes.

To the old rugged cross I will ever be true,
  its shame and reproach gladly bear;
Then He'll call me some day to my home far away,
  where His glory forever I'll share.
So I'll cherish the old rugged cross,
  till my trophies at last I lay down;
I will cling to the old rugged cross,
  and exchange it some day for a crown.

GEORGE BENNARD, 1873–1958

FOR REFLECTION

What is my greatest concern in life—being right, or being righteous?

EVENING READING

It is an important matter for beginners in prayer to start off by becoming detached from every kind of satisfaction and to enter the path solely with the determination to help Christ carry the cross like good cavaliers, who desire to serve their King at no salary since their salary is certain. We should fix our eyes on the true and everlasting kingdom which we are trying to gain. It is very important to keep this kingdom always in mind, especially in the beginning. For afterward it is seen so clearly that rather than striving to keep remembering the short time everything lasts and how everything is nothing and how rest should be considered no more than a trifle, it is necessary to forget these things in order to live.

Detachment From Physical Well-Being

Is any one among you suffering? Let him pray.
Is any cheerful? Let him sing praise.
Is any among you sick? Let him call for the elders of the church, and let them pray over him, anointing him with oil in the name of the Lord; and the prayer of faith will save the sick man, and the Lord will raise him up; and if he has committed sins, he will be forgiven.

JAMES 5:13-15

MORNING READING

It seems to me an imperfection, my Sisters, to be always complaining about light illnesses. If you can tolerate them, don't complain about them. If one has the habit of complaining, it wears everyone out if you have love for one another and there is charity. If someone is truly sick, she should say so and take the necessary remedy. If you do not lose the habit of speaking and complaining about everything—unless you do so to God—you will never finish your lamenting. A fault this body has is that the more comfort we try to give it the more needs it discovers. It's amazing how much comfort it wants; and since in the case of health the need presents itself under the color of some good, however small it may be, the poor soul is deceived and doesn't grow. Oh, you who are free from the great trials of the world, learn how to suffer a little for love of God without having everyone know about it! Abandon yourselves to God, come what may.

Out of my bondage, sorrow and night, Jesus, I come, Jesus, I come
Into Thy freedom, gladness and light, Jesus I come to Thee.
Out of my sickness into Thy health, Out of my want and into Thy
wealth,
Out of my sin and into Thyself, Jesus I come to Thee.

WILLIAM T. SLEEPER, 1819–1904

FOR REFLECTION

How can I abandon myself more fully to His Majesty—in body, soul, and spirit?

EVENING READING

The first thing we must strive for is to rid ourselves of our love for our bodies, for some of us are by nature such lovers of comfort that there is no small amount of work in this area. And we are so fond of our health that it is amazing what a war our bodies cause. Be determined, Sisters, that you came to die for Christ, not to live comfortably for Christ.

Detachment From Excessive Affection

So if there be any encouragement in Christ, any incentive of love, any participation in the Spirit, any affection and sympathy, complete my joy by being of the same mind, having the same love, being in full accord and of one mind. Do nothing from selfishness or conceit, but in humility count others better than yourselves.

PHILIPPIANS 2:1-3

MORNING READING

Those who are interested in perfection have a deep understanding of this excessive love, because little by little it takes away the strength of will to be totally occupied in loving God. It gives rise to the following: failing to love equally all others; feeling sorry about any affront to the friend; desiring possessions so as to give her gifts; looking for time to speak with her, and often so as to tell her that you hold her dear and other trifling things rather than about your love for God. For when love is in the service of His Majesty, the will does not proceed with passion but proceeds by seeking help to conquer other passions.

Better friendship will this be than all the tender words that can be uttered, for these are not used, nor should they be used, in this house; those like, "my life," "my soul," "my only good," and other similar expressions addressed now to one, now to another, of the Sisters. Keep these words of affection for your Spouse, for you must be with Him so much and so alone that you will need to be helped by everything; His Majesty allows us to use these words with Him. But if they are used a lot among ourselves, they will not be so touching when used with the Lord.

What language shall I borrow to thank Thee, dearest Friend,
For this Thy dying sorrow, Thy pity without end?
O make me Thine for ever! And, should I fainting be,
Lord, let me never, never outlive my love to Thee!

ATTRIBUTED TO BERNARD OF CLAIRVAUX, 1091–1153

FOR REFLECTION

"Let us not condescend to allow our wills to be slaves to anyone, save to the One who bought it with His blood."

EVENING READING

Spiritual love seems to imitate that love which the good lover Jesus had for us. Hence these lovers advance so far because they embrace all trials, and the others, without trial, receive benefit from those who love. These lovers cannot in their hearts be insincere with those they love; if they see them deviate from the path or commit some faults they immediately tell them about it.

There is a continual war between the two attitudes these lovers have; on the one hand they go about forgetful of the whole world, taking no account of whether others serve God or not but only keeping account of themselves; on the other hand, with their friends, they have no power to do this, nor is anything covered over; they see the tiniest speck. (Oh fortunate are the souls loved by such as these!)

Building an Eternal "Focus"

Count it all joy, my brethren, when you meet various trials, for you know that the testing of your faith produces steadfastness. And let steadfastness have its full effect, that you may be perfect and complete, lacking in nothing. If any of you lacks wisdom, let him ask God, who gives to all men generously and without reproaching, and it will be given him.

JAMES 1:2-5

MORNING READING

A great aid to going against your will is to bear in mind continually how all is vanity and how quickly everything comes to an end. This helps to remove our attachment to trivia and center it on what will never end. Even though this practice seems to be a weak means, it will strengthen the soul greatly, and the soul will be most careful in very little things. When we begin to become attached to something, we should strive to turn our thoughts from it and bring them back to God—and His Majesty helps. Here true humility can enter the picture because this virtue and the virtue of detachment always go together.

> *Forbid it, Lord, that I should boast*
> *Save in the death of Christ, my God;*
> *All the vain things that charm me most,*
> *I sacrifice them to his blood.*

ISAAC WATTS, 1674–1748

FOR REFLECTION

"O my God! What harm is done in the world by considering our actions of only little importance and by thinking something can be done against You in secret!"

EVENING READING

There are, because of our sins, many persons to whom God has granted favors who through their own fault have fallen back into misery. In the monastery we are free with respect to exterior matters; in interior matters may it please the Lord that we also be free, and may He free us. Guard yourselves, my daughters, from extraneous cares. Remember that there are few dwelling places in this castle in which the devils do not wage battle.

It's true that we cannot live without faults, but at least there should be some change so that they don't take root. If they take root, they will be harder to eradicate and even many others could arise from them. Committing the same fault each day, however small, if we do not make amends for it, is like watering a plant each day. And if one day it is planted and ten more pass by, it can still be easily rooted out. In prayer you must ask help from the Lord, for we of ourselves can do little; rather, we add faults instead of taking them away.

By Faith, Not by Sight ...

The Mystery of the Soul's Best Food

The Lord Reveals Himself in the Eucharist

As they were eating, Jesus took the bread, and blessed, and broke it, and gave it to the disciples and said, "Take, eat; this is my body."
And he took a cup, and when he had given thanks he gave it to them, saying, "Drink of it, all of you; for this is my blood of the covenant, which is poured out for many for the forgiveness of sins."
MATTHEW 26:26-28

MORNING READING

When I approached to receive Communion and recalled that extraordinary majesty I had seen and considered that it was present in the Blessed Sacrament, my hair stood on end; the whole experience seemed to annihilate me. O my Lord! If you did not hide Your grandeur, who would approach so often a union of something so dirty and miserable with such great majesty! May the angels and all creatures praise You, for You so measure things in accordance with our weakness that when we rejoice in Your sovereign favors Your great power does not so frighten us that, as weak and wretched people, we would not dare enjoy them.

At the Lamb's high feast we sing praise to our victorious King.
Who has washed us in the tide flowing from his pierced side;
Praise we him, whose love divine gives his sacred Blood for wine,
Gives his Body for the feast, Christ the victim, Christ the priest.

TRANSLATED FROM LATIN
BY ROBERT CAMPBELL, 1814–1868

FOR REFLECTION

O Lord, give me a fresh vision of Your presence in the Eucharist.
Only say the word, and I shall be healed.

EVENING READING

The will is inclined to love after seeing such countless signs of love;
it would want to repay something; it especially keeps in mind how
this true Lover never leaves it, accompanying it and giving it life
and being. Then the intellect helps it realize that it couldn't find a
better friend, even were it to live for many years, that the whole
world is filled with falsehood, and that so too these joys the devil
gives it are filled with trials, cares, and contradictions. The intellect
tells the soul of its certainty that outside this castle neither security
nor peace will be found, that it should avoid going about to
strange houses since its own is so filled with blessings to be
enjoyed if it wants.

The Soul Expands to Receive the Great Graces of the Lord

But thanks be to God, who in Christ always leads us in triumph, and through us spreads the fragrance of the knowledge of him everywhere.

For we are the aroma of Christ to God among those who are being saved and among those who are perishing, to one a fragrance from death to death, to the other a fragrance from life to life.

2 CORINTHIANS 2:14-16a

MORNING READING

Your breasts are better than wine. Great is this favor, my Spouse; a pleasing feast. Precious wine do You give me, for with one drop alone You make me forget all of creation and go out from creatures and myself, so that I will no longer want the joys and comforts that my sensuality desired up until now. Great is this favor; I did not deserve it.

May our Lord give us understanding or, to put it better, a taste of what the soul's joy is in this state [of contemplation]. Let worldly people worry about their lordships, riches, delights, honors, and food, for even if a person were able to enjoy all these things without the accompanying trials—which is impossible—he would not attain in a thousand years the happiness that in one moment is enjoyed by a soul brought here by the Lord.

Thou, O Christ, art all I want; more than all in Thee I find;
Raise the fallen, cheer the faint, heal the sick and lead the blind.
Just and holy is Thy name, I am all unrighteousness;
False and full of sin I am, Thou art full of truth and grace.

CHARLES WESLEY, 1707–1788

FOR REFLECTION

"May it please His Majesty that I die rather than ever cease to love Him."

EVENING READING

An infant doesn't understand how it grows nor does it know how to get its milk, for without its sucking or doing anything, often the milk is put into its mouth. Likewise, here, the soul is completely ignorant. It knows neither how nor from where that great blessing came to it, nor can it understand. It knows that the blessing is the greatest that can be tasted in life, even if all the delights and pleasures of the world were joined together. It sees that it is nourished and made better and doesn't know when it deserved this. It is instructed in great truths without seeing the Master who teaches it; fortified in virtues and favored by One who knows it well and can do these things for it. It doesn't know what to compare His grace to, unless to the great love a mother has for her child in nourishing and caressing it.

DAY 41
Give Us This Day...

Our Father who art in heaven / Hallowed be thy name.
Thy kingdom come, thy will be done, / On earth as it is in heaven.
Give us this day our daily bread;
And forgive us our debts, / As we also have forgiven our debtors;
And lead us not into temptation, / But deliver us from evil.
MATTHEW 6:9-13

MORNING READING

In no matter how many ways the soul may desire to eat, it will find delight and consolation in the most Blessed Sacrament. (I don't want to think the Lord had in mind the other bread that is used for our bodily needs and nourishment; nor would I want you to have that in mind. The Lord was in the most sublime contemplation. Would He have placed so much emphasis on the petition that He as well as ourselves eat? He is teaching us to set our wills on heavenly things and to ask that we might begin enjoying Him from here below; and would He get us involved in something so base as asking to eat? For once we start worrying about our bodily needs, those of the soul will be forgotten!)

There is no need or trial or persecution that is not easy to suffer if we begin to enjoy the delight and consolation of this sacred bread.

We walk by faith, and not by sight;
No gracious words we hear
From him who spoke as none e'er spoke;
But we believe him near.

HENRY ALFORD, 1810–1871

FOR REFLECTION

"Ask the Father ... to give you your Spouse 'this day' so that you will not be seen in the world without Him."

EVENING READING

Do you think this heavenly food fails to provide sustenance, even for these bodies, that it is not a great medicine even for bodily ills? I know that it is. I know a person with serious illnesses, who often experiences great pain, who through this bread had them taken away as though by a gesture of the hand.

The wonders this most sacred bread effects in those who worthily receive it are well known.

Seeing With the Eyes of Faith

Eight days later, his disciples were again in the house, and Thomas was with them. The doors were shut, but Jesus came and stood among them, and said, "Peace be with you." Then he said to Thomas, "Put your finger here, and see my hands; and put out your hand, and place it in my side; do not be faithless, but believing." Thomas answered him, "My Lord and my God!" Jesus said to him, "Have you believed because you have seen me? Blessed are those who have not seen and yet believe."

JOHN 20:26-29

MORNING READING

If you have to pray to Him by looking at His picture, it would seem to me foolish. You would be leaving the Person Himself in order to look at a picture of Him. Wouldn't it be silly if a person we love very much and of whom we have a portrait came to see us and we stopped speaking with him so as to carry on a conversation with the portrait? Do you want to know when it is very good to have a picture of Christ and when it is a thing in which I find much delight? When He himself is absent, or when by means of a great dryness He wants to make us feel He is absent.

But after receiving the Lord, since you have the Person Himself present, strive to close the eyes of the body and open those of the soul and look into your own heart. For I tell you, and tell you again, and would like to tell you many times that you should acquire the habit of doing this every time you receive Communion and strive to have such a conscience that you will be allowed to enjoy this blessing frequently.

'Tis so sweet to trust in Jesus, Just to take Him at His word
Just to rest upon His promise, Just to know, "Thus saith the Lord."
Jesus, Jesus, how I trust Him! How I've proved Him o'er and o'er!
Jesus, Jesus, precious Jesus! O for grace to trust Him more!

LOUISA M.R. STEAD, 1850–1917

FOR REFLECTION

Open my eyes, Lord. I want to see Jesus.

EVENING READING

If we prepare ourselves to receive Him, He never fails to give in many ways which we do not understand. It is like approaching a fire; even though the fire may be a large one, it will not be able to warm you well if you turn away and hide your hands, though you will still get more heat than you would if you were in a place without one. But it is something else if we desire to approach Him. If the soul is disposed, and if it remains there for a while, it will stay warm for many hours.

In the Shadow of the Bridegroom

As the bridegroom rejoices over the bride,
so shall your God rejoice over you.

ISAIAH 62:5b

MORNING READING

Father John of the Cross, who was giving me the Blessed Sacrament, broke the host to provide for another Sister. His Majesty said to me: "Don't fear, daughter, for no one will be a party to separating you from Me," making me thereby understand that what just happened didn't matter. Then He appeared to me in an imaginative vision, as at other times, very interiorly, and He gave me His right hand and said: "Behold this nail; it is a sign you will be My bride from today on. Until now you have not merited this; from now on not only will you look after My honor as being the honor of your Creator, King, and God, but you will look after it as My true bride. My honor is yours, and yours Mine."

In Thee is gladness amid all sadness, Jesus, sunshine of my heart!
By Thee are given the gifts of heaven, Thou the true Redeemer art!
Our souls Thou wakest, our bonds Thou breakest,
Who trusts Thee surely hath built securely,
He stands forever: Alleluia!

JOHANN LINDEMANN, 1598
TRANSLATED BY CATHERINE WINKWORTH, 1863

FOR REFLECTION

Lord, may I always be ready for my Bridegroom, my garments of righteousness spotless, and my lamp filled with the oil of compassion.

EVENING READING

O souls that practice prayer, taste all these words! How many ways there are of thinking about our God. How different the kinds of food we can make from Him! He is manna, for the taste we get from Him conforms to the taste we prefer. Oh, what heavenly shade this is! And who could say what the Lord reveals from it! I recall what the angels said to the most Blessed Virgin, our Lady: *the power of the Most High will overshadow you.* How fortified will a soul be when the Lord places it in this grandeur! Rightly can it sit down and be assured.

The Holy Spirit must be a mediator between the soul and God, the One who moves it with such ardent desires, for He enkindles it in a supreme fire, which is so near. O Lord, how great are these mercies You show to the soul here! May You be blessed and praised forever, for You are so good a Lover. O my God and my Creator!

Suffer God to Guide Thee ...

The Soul Searches for the Will of God

Two Things the Lord Asks of Us

"Teacher, which is the great commandment in the law?"

And [Jesus] said to him, "You shall love the Lord your God with all your heart, and with all your soul, and with all your mind. This is the great and first commandment. And the second is like it, You shall love your neighbor as yourself. On these two commandments depend all the law and the prophets."

MATTHEW 22:36-40

MORNING READING

The Lord doesn't have to grant us great delights for this union; sufficient is what He has given us in His Son, who would teach us the way. Don't think the matter lies in my being so conformed to the will of God that if my father or brother dies I don't feel it, or that if there are trials or sicknesses I suffer them happily. The Lord asks of us only two things: love of His Majesty and love of our neighbor. These are what we must work for. By observing them with perfection, we do His will and so will be united with Him.

The most certain sign as to whether or not we are observing these two laws is whether we observe well the love of neighbor. We cannot know whether or not we love God, although there are strong indications for recognizing that we do love Him; but we can know whether we love our neighbor. And be certain that the more advanced you will be in the love of God, for the love of His Majesty has for us is so great that to repay us for our love of neighbor He will in a thousand ways increase the love we have for Him. I cannot doubt this.

Take my love, my God, I pour
At Thy feet its treasure store;
Take myself and I will be
Ever, only, all for Thee.

FRANCES R. HAVERGAL, 1874

FOR REFLECTION

Mother Teresa spoke of seeing Jesus "in distressing disguise" in the figures of the poor and sick around her. May we diligently seek a glimpse of His image in those we encounter each day, no matter how dim the reflection.

EVENING READING

The Lord desires intensely that we love him and seek His company, so much so that from time to time He calls us to draw near to Him. These appeals and calls come through words spoken by other good people, or through sermons, or through what is read in good books, or through the many things that are heard and by which God calls, or through illnesses and trials, or also through a truth that He teaches during brief moments we spend in prayer; however lukewarm these moments may be, God esteems them highly.

"And No One Can Take Them From My Hand"

My sheep hear my voice, and I know them, and they follow me; and I give them eternal life, and they shall never perish, and no one shall snatch them out of my hand. My Father, who has given them to me, is greater than all, and no one is able to snatch them out of the Father's hand. I and the Father are one.

JOHN 10:27-30

MORNING READING

Let's suppose that the senses and faculties [of the people already in the castle] have gone outside and have walked for days and years with strangers—enemies of the well-being of the castle. Having seen their perdition, they've already begun to approach the castle even though they may not manage to remain inside because the habit of doing so is difficult to acquire. Once the great King, who is in the center dwelling place of this castle, sees their goodwill, He desires in His wonderful mercy to bring them back to Him. Like a good shepherd, with a whistle so gentle that even they themselves almost fail to hear it, He makes them recognize His voice and stops them from going so far astray so that they will return to their dwelling place. And this shepherd's whistle has such power that they abandon the exterior things in which they were estranged from Him and enter the castle.

Softly and tenderly Jesus is calling, calling for you and for me;
See on the portals He's waiting and watching, watching for you
    and for me.
Come home, come home, ye who are weary come home;
Earnestly, tenderly Jesus is calling, calling, O sinner, come home!

WILL L. THOMPSON, 1880

FOR REFLECTION

"You already know that God is everywhere. It's obvious, then, that where the king is there is his court; in sum, wherever God is, there is heaven."

EVENING READING

Some persons have turned away from One who with so much love wanted to be their friend and proved it by deeds. The devil tries much harder for a soul of this kind than for very many to whom the Lord does not grant these favors. For such a soul can do a great deal of harm to the devil by getting others to follow it, and it could be of great benefit to God's Church. And even though the devil may have no other reason than to see who it is to whom His Majesty shows particular love, that's sufficient for him to wear himself out trying to lead the soul to perdition. So these souls suffer much combat, and if they go astray, they stray much more than do others. From pride and vainglory may God deliver you.

DAY 46

The Wine Cellar of God's Abundant Will

Some went down to the sea in ships, doing business
on the great waters;
they saw the deeds of the Lord, his wondrous works in the deep.
For he commanded, and raised the stormy wind,
which lifted up the waves of the sea....
Then they cried to the Lord in their trouble;
he made the storm be still, and the waves of the sea were hushed.
Then they were glad because they had quiet,
and he brought them to their desired haven.

PSALM 107:23-25, 28-30

MORNING READING

[Editor's note: In this passage St. Teresa reminds us of the power of God to draw and keep a soul deeper into intimacy with Him. His Majesty does not overpower the unwilling, but gently and firmly draws His cords of love around those who are submitted to His will.] You have heard the bride say in the Song of Songs: *He brought me into the wine cellar.* And it doesn't say that she went. And it says also that she went looking about in every part of the city for her Beloved. I understand this union to be the wine cellar where the Lord wishes to place us when He desires and as He desires. But however great the effort we make to do so, we cannot enter. His Majesty must place us there and enter Himself into the center of our soul. And that He may show His marvels more clearly He doesn't want our will to have any part to play, for it has been entirely surrendered to Him.

Jesus, lover of my soul, let me to Thy bosom fly,
While the nearer waters roll, while the tempest still is high!
Hide me, O my Savior, hide—till the storm of life is past
Safe into the haven guide, O receive my soul at last!

CHARLES WESLEY, 1707–1788

FOR REFLECTION

It is not in the flurries of life, but in the calm after the storm, that God's voice can best be heard.

EVENING READING

The one who thinks less and has less desire to act does more. What we must do is beg like the needy poor before a rich and great emperor, and then lower our eyes and wait with humility. When through His secret paths it seems we understand that He hears us, then it is good to be silent since He has allowed us to remain near Him.

Resignation to the Will of God

Now may the God of peace who brought again from the dead our Lord Jesus, the great shepherd of the sheep, by the blood of the eternal covenant, equip you with everything good that you may do his will, working in you that which is pleasing in his sight, through Jesus Christ; to whom be glory forever and ever. Amen.

HEBREWS 13:20-21

MORNING READING

After a year and a half in the convent school, I began to recite many vocal prayers and to seek that all commend me to God so that He might show me the state in which I was to serve Him. But still I had no desire to be a nun, and I asked God not to give me this vocation; although I also feared marriage.

By the end of this period of time in which I stayed there I was more favorable to the thought of being a nun, although not at that house. During this time, although I did not neglect my spiritual improvement, the Lord was more determined to prepare me for the state that was better for me. He sent me a serious illness so that I had to return to my father's house. Although my will did not completely incline to being a nun, I saw that the religious life was the best and safest state, and so little by little I decided to force myself to accept it.

Sing, pray and keep His ways unswerving;
  in all thy labor faithful be,
And trust His word; though undeserving,
  thou yet shall find it true for thee;
God never will forsake in need
The soul that trusts in Him indeed.

GEORG NEUMARK, 1641
TRANSLATED BY CATHERINE WINKWORTH, 1855

FOR REFLECTION

"When the Lord wishes the work to be done He will give us the wherewithal."

EVENING READING

Well, see here, daughters, what He gave to the one He loved most. By that we understand what His will is. For these are His gifts in this world. He gives according to the love He bears us: to those He loves more, He gives more of these gifts; to those He loves less, He gives less. And He gives according to the courage He sees in each and the love each has for His Majesty. He will see that whoever loves Him much will be able to suffer much for Him; whoever loves Him little will be capable of little.

The Example of the Martyrs

"Who are these, clothed in white robes, and whence have them come?"

And he said to me, "These are they who have come out of the great tribulation; they have washed their robes and made them white in the blood of the Lamb.... The Lamb in the midst of the throne will be their shepherd, and he will guide them to springs of living water; and God will wipe away every tear from their eyes."

REVELATION 7:13-14, 17

MORNING READING

On another day the Lord told me this: "Do you think, daughter, that merit lies in enjoyment? No, rather it lies in working and suffering and loving. Haven't you heard that St. Paul rejoiced in heavenly joys only once and that he suffered often. Look at my whole life filled with suffering, and only in the incident on Mount Tabor do you hear about my joy. The great saints ... spent long periods without any spiritual consolation.

"Believe, daughter, that My Father gives greater trials to anyone whom He loves more; and love responds to these. How can I show you greater love than by desiring for you what I have desired for Myself? Behold these wounds, for your sufferings have never reached this point. Suffering is the way of truth."

Lo! the apostolic train join Thy sacred name to hallow;
Prophets swell the glad refrain,
  and the white-robed martyrs follow,
And from morn to set of sun,
Through the Church the song goes on.

ATTRIBUTED TO IGNACE FRANZ, C. 1774
TRANSLATED BY CLARENCE A. WALWORTH, 1853

FOR REFLECTION

"Those who are going to be saved will always have trials of one kind or another, and God does not allow us to choose."

EVENING READING

In weeping be my joy, my rest in fright,
In sorrowing my serenity, my wealth in losing all.
Amid storms be my love, in the wound my delight.
My life in death, in rejection my favor.
In poverty be my riches, my triumph in struggling,
Rest in laboring, in sadness my contentment.
In darkness be my light, my greatness in the lowly place,
My way on the short road, in the cross my glory.
In humiliation be my honor, my balm in suffering
Increase in my wanting, in losing my gain.
My fullness be in hunger, in fearing my hope,
My rejoicing in fear, in grieving my delight.
In forgetting be my memory, humiliation my exalting
In lowliness my repute, affronts my victory.
My laurels be in contempt, in afflictions my fondness,
My dignity a lowly nook, in solitude my esteem.
In Christ be my trust, my affection in Him alone,
In His weariness my vigor, my repose in His imitation.
My strength is founded here, in Him alone my surety,
My integrity's proof, in His likeness my purity.

Nearer, My God, to Thee ...

*Enduring Hardship to
Strengthen the Soul*

Take Up the Cross of Your Spouse!

For his sake I have suffered the loss of all things, and count them as refuse, in order that I might gain Christ and be found in him, not having a righteousness of my own, based on law, but that which is through faith in Christ, the righteousness from God that depends on faith; that I may know him and the power of his resurrection, and may share his sufferings, becoming like him in his death, that if possible I may attain the resurrection from the dead.

PHILIPPIANS 3:8b-11

MORNING READING

They say that for a woman to be a good wife toward her husband she must be sad when he is sad, and joyful when he is joyful, even though she may not be so. The Lord, without deception, truly acts in such a way with us. He is the one who submits. If you are joyful, look at Him as risen. The brilliance! The beauty! The majesty! How victorious! If you are experiencing trials or are sad, behold Him on the way to the garden. Or burdened with the cross. He will look at you with those eyes so beautiful and compassionate, filled with tears; He will forget His sorrows so as to console you in yours, merely because you yourselves go to Him to be consoled, and you turn your head to look at Him.

Are You so in need, my Lord and my Love, that You would want to receive such poor company as mine, for I see by Your expression that You have been consoled by me? If it's true, Lord, that You want to endure everything for me, what is this that I suffer for You? Of what am I complaining? Wherever You go, I will go; whatever you suffer, I will suffer.

Nearer, my God, to Thee, nearer to Thee!
Even though it be a cross that raiseth me;
Still all my song shall be, nearer my God, to Thee.
Nearer, my God, to Thee, nearer to Thee!

SARAH F. ADAMS, 1805–1848

FOR REFLECTION

"God gives no more than what can be endured; and His Majesty gives patience first."

EVENING READING

[Editor's note: St. Teresa's admonishment to her sisters offers comfort to all those who must suffer.] Take up your cross, daughters. In stumbling, in falling with your Spouse, do not withdraw from the cross or abandon it. Consider carefully the fatigue with which He walks and how much greater His trials are than the trials you suffer, however great you may want to paint them and no matter how much you grieve over them. You will come out consoled because you will see that they are something to be laughed at when compared to those of the Lord.

DAY 50
Trusting God's Provision in All Things

God is our refuge and strength, a very present help in trouble.
Therefore we will not fear though the earth should change, though
  the mountains shake in the heart of the sea....
"Be still, and know that I am God. I am exalted among the
  nations, I am exalted in the earth!"
The Lord of hosts is with us; the God of Jacob is our refuge.

PSALM 46:1-2, 10-11

MORNING READING

There is no remedy in this tempest but to wait for the mercy of God. For at an unexpected time, with one word alone or a chance happening, He so quickly calms the storm that it seems there had not been even as much as a cloud in that soul, and it remains filled with sunlight and much more consolation. And like one who has escaped from a dangerous battle and been victorious, it comes out praising our Lord; for it was He who fought for the victory.

> *When peace like a river, attendeth my way,*
> *When sorrows like sea-billows roll—*
> *Whatever my lot, Thou hast taught me to say,*
> *It is well, it is well with my soul.*

HORATIO G. SPAFFORD, 1828–1888

FOR REFLECTION

"O my powerful God, how sublime are your secrets, and how different spiritual things are from all that is visible and understandable here below!"

EVENING READING

His Majesty gives strength to the one He sees has need of it. He defends these souls in all things; when they are persecuted and criticized He answers for them as He did for the Magdalene—if not through words, through deeds. And in the very end, before they die, He will pay for everything at once, as you will now see. May He be blessed forever, and may all creatures praise Him, amen.

The Gift of Pain

For what credit is it, if when you do wrong and are beaten for it
you take it patiently? But if when you do right and suffer for it
you take it patiently, you have God's approval. For to this you have
been called, because Christ also suffered for you, leaving you an
example, that you should follow in his steps.

1 PETER 2:20-21

MORNING READING

It has already been seen through experience the great gain and
progress that comes by suffering for God. Very seldom does God
give such great gifts [as the consolations of true contemplation],
save to persons who have willingly undergone many trials for Him.
As I have said, the trials of contemplatives are great, and so the
Lord looks for contemplatives among people who have been
tested. [Through their suffering] they will gain more graces and
perpetual favors from His Majesty than they would in ten years
through trials they might wish to undertake on their own. Just as
others prize gold and jewels, they prize trials and desire them; they
know that these latter are what will make them rich.

Day by day, and with each passing moment,
strength I find to meet my trials here;
Trusting in my Father's wise bestowment,
I've no cause for worry or for fear.
He whose heart is kind beyond all measure
gives unto each day what He deems best—
Lovingly, its part of pain and pleasure,
mingling toil with peace and rest.

LINA SANDELL BERG , 1832–1903
TRANSLATED BY ANDREW L. SKOOG, 1856–1934

FOR REFLECTION

"Disappointment will pass away, as everything in this life passes away, and, when I remember that, I find things, however unpleasant, easy to bear."

EVENING READING

If suffering for love's sake can give such wondrous delight?
What joy will gazing on You be?

What will it be beholding the Majesty eternal
Since Andrew, seeing the cross, was so filled with rejoicing?
Oh, how can it be wanting,
Delight in suffering's midst!
What joy will gazing on You be?...

O cross, wood so precious, majestic and grand!
Once greatly despised, now espoused to God,
With rejoicing I come, unworthy to love you.
What joy will gazing on You be?

Those God Loves, He Disciplines

*"My son, do not regard lightly the discipline of the Lord, nor lose
courage when you are punished by him. For the Lord disciplines
him whom he loves, and chastises every son whom he receives." It is
for discipline that you have to endure. God is treating you as sons.*

HEBREWS 12:5b-7a

MORNING READING

To think that He admits into His intimate friendship people who
live in comfort and without trials is foolish. I am very certain that
God gives contemplatives much greater trials. Thus, since He
leads them along a rough and uneven path and at times they think
they are lost and must return to begin again, His Majesty needs to
give them sustenance, and not water but wine so that in their
inebriation they will not understand what they are suffering and
will be able to endure it.

I have been thinking of a saint I knew in Ávila [The Venerable
Maridíaz]—for it was quite clear that she was living the life of a
saint. She had given away everything she had for God's sake, till
she had nothing left but the blanket which she used to cover
herself with and then she gave that away too. Immediately God
sent her a period of the severest interior trials and aridities,
whereupon she began to complain bitterly and said: "Are You like
that, Lord? You have left me with nothing and now You are
forsaking me too?" His Majesty *is* like that, my daughter. He
rewards great services with trials, and there can be no better
reward, for out of trials springs love for God.

A wonderful Savior is Jesus my Lord,
   a wonderful Savior to me;
He hideth my soul in the cleft of the rock,
   where rivers of pleasure I see.
He hideth my soul in the cleft of the rock
   that shadows a dry, thirsty land;
He hideth my life in the depths of His love,
   and covers me there with His hand.

FANNY J. CROSBY, 1820–1915

FOR REFLECTION

"Knowing how weak we are, He tempers our sufferings to our strength, and does everything for our good."

EVENING READING

I know a person who cannot truthfully say that from the time the Lord began forty years ago to grant the favor that was mentioned she spent even one day without pains and other kinds of suffering (from lack of bodily health, I mean) and other great trials. Others, who have not offended our Lord so much, will be led by another path. But I would always choose the path of suffering, if only to imitate our Lord Jesus Christ if there were no other gain; especially, since there are so many other benefits.

Forbearing the Shortcomings of Others

*Blessed are those who are persecuted for righteousness' sake, for
theirs is the kingdom of heaven.*

*Blessed are you when men revile you and persecute you and utter
all kinds of evil against you falsely on my account.*

*Rejoice and be glad, for your reward is great in heaven,
for so men persecuted the prophets who were before you.*

MATTHEW 5:10-11

MORNING READING

Fix your eyes on the Crucified and everything will become small
for you. If His Majesty showed us His love by means of such
works and frightful torments, how is it you want to please Him
only with words? Do you know what it means to be truly spiritual?
It means becoming the slaves of God. Marked with His brand,
which is that of the cross, spiritual persons, because now they have
given Him their liberty, can be sold by Him as slaves of everyone,
as He was.

Be still, my soul — the Lord is on thy side!
Bear patiently the cross of grief or pain;
Leave to thy God to order and provide—
In every change He faithful will remain.
Be still, my soul—thy best, thy heavenly Friend
Through thorny ways leads to a joyful end.

KATHARINA VON SCHLEGEL, 1697–?
TRANSLATED BY JANE L. BORTHWICK, 1813–1897

FOR REFLECTION

"I think it does no harm if, in the midst of our prosperity, God sends a little adversity, as that is the way by which He has led all His elect."

EVENING READING

There is nothing annoying that is not suffered easily by those who love one another. And if this commandment were observed in the world as it should be, I think such love would be very helpful for the observance of the other commandments. But, because of either excess or defect, we never reach the point of observing this commandment perfectly.

Jesus, Lover of My Soul ...

The Soul's Eternal Longing for God

Dying to Self:
A Lesson From the Silkworm

If then you have been raised with Christ, seek the things that are above, where Christ is, seated at the right hand of God. Set your minds on things that are above, not on things that are on earth. For you have died, and your life is hid with Christ in God.

COLOSSIANS 3:1-3

MORNING READING

[Editor's note: In her discourse on the fifth room of the soul's castle, St. Teresa compares the spiritually maturing soul to that of a silkworm.] The silkworms come from seeds about the size of grains of pepper. When the warm weather comes and the leaves begin to appear on the mulberry tree, the seeds start to live, for they are dead until then. The worms nourish themselves on mulberry leaves, spinning the silk and making some thick little cocoons in which they enclose themselves. The silkworm, which is fat and ugly, then dies, and a little white butterfly, which is very pretty, comes forth from the cocoon.

This silkworm [of the soul], then, starts to live when by the heat of the Holy Spirit it begins to benefit through the general help given to us all by God and through the remedies left by Him to His Church, by going to confession, reading good books, and hearing sermons, which are the remedies of the soul. It then begins to live and to sustain itself by these things, and by good meditations, until it is grown. Once the silkworm is grown, it begins to spin the silk and build the house wherein it will die. This house is Christ. His Majesty Himself, as He does in this prayer of union, becomes the dwelling place we build for ourselves.

Loved with everlasting love, led by grace that love to know—
Spirit, breathing from above, Thou hast taught me it is so!
O this full and perfect peace, O this transport all divine—
In a love which cannot cease, I am His and He is mine.

WADE ROBINSON, 1838–1877

FOR REFLECTION

Even things that are spiritually beneficial ("remedies of the soul") can deter us from real spiritual growth if we lose our true focus and become comfortable with the spiritual "status quo." In what areas is God challenging you to become less of a silkworm—and more of a butterfly?

EVENING READING

O my delight, Lord of all created things and my God! How long must I wait to see You? What remedy do You provide for one who finds so little on earth that might give some rest apart from You? What shall I do, my God? Should I, perhaps, desire not to desire You? Oh, my God and my Creator, You wound and You do not supply the medicine; You kill, leaving one with more life! In sum, my Lord, being powerful You do what You will. Well, my God, do You want so despicable a worm to suffer these contradictions? Let it be so, my God, since You desire it, for I desire nothing but to love You.

God Multiplies the Efforts of Those Who Try to Please Him

Set your heart right and be steadfast, and do not be hasty in time of calamity. Cleave to him and do not depart, that you may be honored at the end of your life. Accept whatever is brought upon you, and in changes that humble you be patient. For gold is tested in the fire, and acceptable men in the furnace of humiliation. Trust in him, and he will help you; make your ways straight, and hope in him.

SIRACH 2:2-6

MORNING READING

It seems I'm saying that we can build up God and take Him away since I say that He is the dwelling place and we ourselves can build it so as to place ourselves in it. And, indeed, we can! Not that we can take God away or build Him up, but we can take away from ourselves and build up, as do these little silkworms. For we will not have finished doing all that we can in this work when, to the little we do, which is nothing, God will unite Himself, with His greatness, and give it such high value that the Lord Himself will become the reward of this work. Thus, since it was He who paid the highest price, His Majesty wants to join our little labors with the great ones He suffered so that all the work may become one.

Therefore, courage, my daughters! Let's be quick to do this work and weave this little cocoon by getting rid of our self-love and self-will, our attachment to any earthly thing. Let it die; let this silkworm die, as it does in completing what it was created to do! And you will see how we see God, as well as ourselves placed inside His greatness, as is this little silkworm within its cocoon.

There's a wideness in God's mercy like the wideness of the sea;
There's a kindness in God's justice which is more than liberty.
There is plentiful redemption in the blood that has been shed;
There is joy for all the members in the sorrows of the Head.

FREDERICK W. FABER, 1814–1863

FOR REFLECTION

St. Teresa admonishes us, "What do you think His will is, daughters? That we be completely perfect." When our Heavenly Father looks at us and sees Jesus in us, that is perfection indeed.

EVENING READING

I often marveled to think of the great goodness of God, and my soul delighted in seeing His amazing magnificence and mercy. May He be blessed by all, for I have seen clearly that He does not fail to repay, even in this life, every good desire. As miserable and imperfect as my deeds were, this Lord of mine improved and perfected them and gave them value, and the evils and sins He then hid.

Longing for Intimacy With God, Now and in Eternity

Oh, that you would kiss me with the kisses of your mouth!
For your love is better than wine, your anointing oils are fragrant,
Your name is oil poured out; therefore the maidens love you.
Draw me after you, let us make haste.
The king has brought me into his chambers.

SONG OF SOLOMON 1:2-4a

MORNING READING

Let Him kiss me with the kiss of His mouth ... O my Lord and my God, and what words are these that a worm speaks them to its Creator! May You be blessed, Lord, for in so many ways have You taught us! But who will dare, my King, utter these words without Your permission? The thought is frightening, and so it will be frightening that I tell anyone to utter them.

I confess that the passage has many meanings. But the soul that is enkindled with a love that makes it mad desires nothing else than to say these words. Indeed, the Lord does not forbid her to say them.

God help me! Why are we surprised? Isn't the deed more admirable? Do we not approach the most Blessed Sacrament? And I was even wondering if the bride was asking for this favor that Christ afterward gave us. I also wondered whether she was asking for that union so great that God became man, for that friendship that he effected with the human race. Obviously a kiss is the sign of great peace and friendship among two persons. May the Lord help us understand how many kinds of peace there are.

Jesus, the very thought of Thee with sweetness fills my breast;
But sweeter far Thy face to see and in Thy presence rest.
Nor voice can sing, nor heart can frame, nor can the mem'ry find
A sweeter sound than Thy blest name, O Savior of mankind.

BERNARD OF CLAIRVAUX, 1091–1153

FOR REFLECTION

"What better thing can we ask for than what I ask You for, my Lord; that You give me this peace 'with the kiss of Your mouth'?"

EVENING READING

O Lord of my soul and my good! When a soul is determined to love You by doing what it can to leave all and occupy itself in this divine love, why don't You desire that it enjoy soon the ascent to the possession of perfect love?... The whole fault is ours if we don't soon reach the enjoyment of a dignity so great, for the perfect attainment of this true love of God brings with it every blessing. We are so miserly and so slow in giving ourselves entirely to God that since His Majesty does not desire that we enjoy something as precious as this without paying a high price, we do not fully prepare ourselves.

There is nothing on earth with which one can buy so wonderful a blessing. But if we do what we can to avoid becoming attached to any earthly thing and let all our care and concern be with heavenly things, and if within a short time we prepare ourselves completely, as some of the saints did, I believe without a doubt that in a very short time this blessing will be given to us.

St. Teresa Illustrates "Union With God"

His gifts were that ... we all attain to the unity of the faith and of the knowledge of the Son of God, to mature manhood, to the measure of the stature of the fullness of Christ;... Speaking the truth in love, we are to grow up in every way into him who is the head, into Christ, from whom the whole body, joined and knit together by every joint with which it is supplied, when each part is working properly, makes bodily growth and upbuilds itself in love.

EPHESIANS 4:11, 13, 15-16

MORNING READING

The prayer of union does not yet reach the stage of spiritual betrothal. Here below when two people are to be engaged, there is discussion about whether they are alike, whether they love each other, and whether they might meet together so as to become more satisfied with each other. So, too, in the case of this union with God, the agreement has been made, and this soul is well informed about the goodness of her Spouse and determined to do His will in everything and in as many ways as she sees might make Him happy. And His Majesty, as one who understands clearly whether these things about His betrothed are so, is happy with her. As a result He grants this mercy, for He desired her to know Him more and that they might meet together, as they say, and be united.

Here, O my Lord, I see Thee face to face,
Here would I touch and handle things unseen,
Here grasp with firmer hand eternal grace,
And all my weariness upon Thee lean.

HORATIUS BONAR, 1808–1889

FOR REFLECTION

What gifts have you given me that I could use more fully for you today, my Lord?

EVENING READING

Union is like the joining of two wax candles to such an extent that the flame coming from them is but one, or that the wick, the flame, and the wax are all one. But afterward one candle can be easily separated from the other and there are two candles; the same holds for the wick. In the spiritual marriage the union is like what we have when rain falls from the sky into a river or fount; all is water, for the rain that fell from heaven cannot be divided or separated from the water of the river. Or it is like what we have when a little stream enters the sea, there is no means of separating the two. Or, like the bright light entering a room through two different windows; although the streams of light are separate when entering the room, they become one.

Perhaps this is what St. Paul means in saying *He that is joined or united to the Lord becomes one spirit with him.* And he also says: *For me to live is Christ, and to die is gain.*

The Butterfly Emerges: Holy Restlessness

Here is a call for the endurance of the saints, those who keep the commandments of God and the faith of Jesus. And I heard a voice from heaven saying, "Write this: Blessed are the dead who die in the Lord henceforth."

"Blessed indeed," says the Spirit, "that they may rest from their labors, for their deeds follow them!"

REVELATION 14:12-13

MORNING READING

When the soul is truly dead to the world, a little white butterfly comes forth. Oh, greatness of God! How transformed the soul is when it comes out of this prayer after having been placed within the greatness of God and so closely joined with Him for a little while. Truly, the soul doesn't recognize itself. It sees within itself a desire to praise the Lord; it would want to dissolve and die a thousand deaths for Him. There are the strongest desires for penance, for solitude, and that all might know God; and great pain comes to it when it sees that He is offended.

Oh, now, to see the restlessness of this little butterfly, even though it has never been quieter and calmer in its life it doesn't know where to alight and rest. It no longer has any esteem for the works it did while a worm, which was to weave the cocoon little by little; it now has wings. How can it be happy walking step by step when it can fly?

O the deep, deep love of Jesus, love of every love the best!
'Tis an ocean vast of blessing, 'tis a haven sweet of rest.
O the deep, deep love of Jesus, 'tis a heav'n of heav'ns to me;
And it lifts me up to glory, for it lifts me up to Thee.

TREVOR FRANCIS, 1834–1925

FOR REFLECTION

When even good intentions cause me to run ahead of You, Lord, catch me in your great butterfly net and draw me close to Your side.

EVENING READING

Oh, poor little butterfly, bound with so many chains which do not let you fly where you would like! Have pity on it, my God! Ordain that it might somehow fulfill its desires for your honor and glory. You have the power, Lord, to make the great sea and the large river Jordan roll back and allow the children of Israel to pass. Yet, do not take pity on this little butterfly! Helped by your strength, it can suffer many trials; it is determined to do so and desires to suffer them.

Extend Your powerful arm, Lord, that this soul might not spend its life in things so base. Let Your grandeur appear in a creature so feminine and lowly, whatever the cost to her, so that the world may know that this grandeur is not hers at all and may praise You. This praise is what she desires, and she would give a thousand lives—if she had that many—if one soul were to praise You a little more through her; and she would consider such lives very well spent.

Rapture

When I saw him, I fell at his feet as though dead. But he laid his right hand upon me, saying, "Fear not, I am the first and the last, and the living one; I died, and behold I am alive for evermore, and I have the keys of Death and Hades. Now write what you see, what is and what is to take place hereafter...."

REVELATION 1:17-19

MORNING READING

I tell you there is need for more courage [to be married to the King of heaven] than you think. You will see what His Majesty does to conclude this betrothal, which I understand comes about when He gives the soul raptures that draw it out of its senses. For if it were to see itself so near this great majesty while in its senses, it would perhaps die. I want to put down here some kinds of rapture that I've come to understand.

One kind of rapture is that in which the soul even though not in prayer is touched by some word it remembers or hears about God. It seems that His Majesty from the interior of the soul makes the spark we mentioned increase, for He is moved with compassion in seeing the soul suffer so long a time from its desire. All burnt up, the soul is renewed like the phoenix, and one can devoutly believe that its faults are pardoned. Now that it is so pure, the Lord joins it with Himself, without anyone understanding what is happening except these two; nor does the soul itself understand in a way that can afterward be explained.

Praise to the Lord, the Almighty, the King of creation!
O my soul, praise Him, for He is thy health and salvation!
All ye who hear, now to His temple draw near;
Join me in glad adoration!

JOACHIM NEANDER, 1680
TRANSLATED BY CATHERINE WINKWORTH, 1863

FOR REFLECTION

"Some visions are so sublime that it's not fitting for those who live on this earth to have the further understanding necessary to explain them."

EVENING READING

One day after receiving Communion, it seemed most clear to me that our Lord sat beside me; and He began to console me with great favors, and He told me among other things: "See Me here, daughter, for it is I; give Me your hands." And it seemed He took them and placed them in His side and said: "Behold my wounds. You are not without Me. This short life is passing away."

From certain things He told me, I understood that after He ascended to heaven He never came down to earth to commune with anyone except in the most Blessed Sacrament.

153

Wounds of Love:
Consumed by Love for God

And I said, "Woe is me! For I am lost; for I am a man of unclean lips, and I dwell in the midst of a people of unclean lips; for my eyes have seen the King, the Lord of hosts!"

Then flew one of the seraphim to me, having in his hand a burning coal which he had taken with tongs from the altar. And he touched my mouth, and said: "Behold, this has touched your lips; your guilt is taken away, and your sin forgiven." And I heard the voice of the Lord saying, "Whom shall I send, and who will go for us?" Then I said, "Here am I! Send me!"

ISAIAH 6:5-8

MORNING READING

[In a vision] I saw close to me toward my left side an angel in bodily form. The angel was not large but small; he was very beautiful, and his face was so aflame that he seemed to be one of those very sublime angels that appear to be all afire. I saw in his hands a large golden dart and at the end of the iron tip there appeared to be a little fire. It seemed to me this angel plunged the dart several times into my heart and that it reached deep within me. When he drew it out, I thought he was carrying off with him the deepest part of me; and he left me all on fire with great love of God.

The pain is not bodily but spiritual, although the body doesn't fail to share in some of it, and even a great deal. The loving exchange that takes place between the soul and God is so sweet that I beg Him in His goodness to give a taste of this love to anyone who thinks I am lying.

Crown Him with many crowns, the Lamb upon His throne.
Hark! How the heav'nly anthem drowns all music but its own.
Awake, my soul, and sing of Him who died for thee,
And hail Him as thy matchless King through all eternity.

MATTHEW BRIDGES, 1851
AND GODFREY THRING, 1874

FOR REFLECTION

When my soul comes in contact with Your Spirit, Lord, give me the courage not to pull away.

EVENING READING

O delight of angels, when I see this I desire to be completely consumed in loving You! Oh, what a good friend You make, my Lord! How You proceed by favoring and enduring. You wait for the others to adapt to Your nature, and in the meanwhile You put up with theirs! You take into account, my Lord, the times when they love You, and in one instant of repentance You forget their offenses.

NOTES

INTRODUCTION:

1. *The Way of Perfection* (3.7)
2. *Meditations on the Song of Songs* (Introduction, 209–10)
3. *The Interior Castle* (4.2.2–4)

READINGS:

1. *The Interior Castle* (4.2.3–4, 10); *The Foundations* (1.4)
2. *Life* (14.1–2; 16.1; 18.1–5)
3. *The Way of Perfection* (24.2–4; 25.3); *The Interior Castle* (6.10.2)
4. *The Way of Perfection* (22.4, 6; 22.7)
5. *The Interior Castle* (1.1.6); *The Way of Perfection* (24.5; 28.2); *The Interior Castle* (2.1.7–8)
6. *The Way of Perfection* (23.2, 26.1); *Letters* (Letter 209, To P. Jerónimo Gracián; from Ávila, December 1577 (?), 509); *The Way of Perfection* (16.9–10)
7. *The Way of Perfection* (4.2); *Letters* (Letter 59, To Don Teutonio de Braganza, Salamanca; from Segovia, July 3, 1574; 147–48)
8. *The Way of Perfection* (40.1–3; 41.1); *Life* (40.1)
9. *Life* (28.1; 25.17); *Soliloquies* (17.3–4)
10. *Spiritual Testimonies* (13.1); *The Interior Castle* (6.9.4–5; 7.4.3)
11. *The Interior Castle* (1.1.1-2; 1.1.5-7; Epilogue 2)
12. *The Way of Perfection* (17.4-5); *The Interior Castle* (7.4.12)
13. *Meditations on the Song of Songs* (7.1-3); *Life* (21.5)
14. *The Way of Perfection* (1.1-2); *The Interior Castle* (7.4.15)
15. *The Way of Perfection* (4.4); *Life* (31.20-21)

16. *The Way of Perfection* (28.9-11); *The Interior Castle* (6.10.6); *Life* (11.6)

17. *The Way of Perfection* (36.7; 41.7; 36.2)

18. *Life* (2.2-3; 2.5); *The Way of Perfection* (5.3.12); *The Way of Perfection* (41.4-7)

19. *The Interior Castle* (5.4.9-10; 6.6.9)

20. *Life* (14.9; 11.7); *The Interior Castle* (5.1.2)

21. *The Interior Castle* (1.2.8; 4.1.9)

22. *Meditations on the Song of Songs* (2.23-25); *Spiritual Testimonies* (24.1)

23. *The Way of Perfection* (39.4); *The Interior Castle* (6.7.4)

24. *Meditations on the Song of Songs* (Introduction, 210-11); *Letters* (Letter 408, To P. Nicolás de Jesús María (Doria); from Burgos, March 1582 (?), 920); *The Way of Perfection* (39.2)

25. *Life* (20.28-29; 19.2); *The Interior Castle* (6.5.10-11)

26. *Life* (13.15; 11.12); *Letters* (Letter 78a, To M. María Bautista, Valladolid; from Seville, August 28, 1575, 193); *The Way of Perfection* (7.7-8)

27. *The Way of Perfection* (19.2; 19.14-15; 20.2; 21.1)

28. *The Way of Perfection* (19.3-9); *The Interior Castle* (1.2.2-3)

29. *Meditations on the Song of Songs* (2.1-3; 3.1)

30. *Life* (8.2; 11.4)

31. *The Interior Castle* (2.1.3-4), *The Way of Perfection* (16.2, 6-7)

32. *Life* (18.9); *Letters* (Letter 66, To Don Antonio Gaytán, Alba de Tormes; from Valladolid, December 1574, 162; Letter 264, To the Discalced Carmelite nuns of Seville; from Ávila, January 31, 1579, 630)

33. *Meditations on the Song of Songs* (2.8, 2.9-10); *The Way of Perfection* (2.1); *Letters* (Letter 129, To Don Lorenzo de

Capeda, Ávila; from Toledo, November 1576, 333-34).

34. *The Way of Perfection* (9.2-5); *Letters* (Letter 156, To
    Don Diego de Guzmán y Cepeda, Ávila; from Toledo,
    December 1576, 387-89)

35. *The Way of Perfection* (13.1; 15.5); *Life* (15.11)

36. *The Way of Perfection* (11.1-3; 10.5)

37. *The Way of Perfection* (4.5-8; 7.8; 7.4)

38. *The Way of Perfection* (10.2-3); *Life* (2.7); *The Interior Castle*
    (1.2.15); *Meditations on the Song of Songs* (2.18)

39. *Life* (38.19); *The Interior Castle* (2.1.4)

40. *Meditations on the Song of Songs* (4.5-7); *Life* (5.11)

41. *The Way of Perfection* (34.2-3, 6)

42. *The Way of Perfection* (34.11-12; 35.1)

43. *Spiritual Testimonies* (31.1); *Meditations on the Song of Songs*
    (5.2, 5)

44. *The Interior Castle* (5.3.7-8; 2.1.2-3)

45. *The Interior Castle* (4.3.2); *The Way of Perfection* (28.2); *The
    Interior Castle* (4.3.10)

46. *The Interior Castle* (5.2.12; 4.3.5)

47. *Life* (3.2-3); *Letters* (Letter 70, To Don Teutonio de
    Braganza, Salamanca; from Valladolid, January 6, 1575,
    168); *The Way of Perfection* (32.7)

48. *Spiritual Testimonies* (32.1); *Letters* (Letter 36, To Doña
    Juana de Ahumada; from the Convent of the Incarnation,
    Ávila, March 1572, 106); *Poetry* "For the Profession of
    Isabel de los Angeles (402.26)

49. *The Way of Perfection* (26.4-6); *The Interior Castle* (6.1.6);
    The Way of Perfection (26.7)

50. *The Interior Castle* (6.1.10; 6.2.3; 6.11.12)

51. *The Way of Perfection* (36.8-9); *Letters* (Letter 62, To
    M. María Bautista, Valladolid; from Segovia, September 11,

1574, 153); *Poetry* "To Saint Andrew" (397.21)

52. *The Way of Perfection* (18.2); *Letters* (Letter 403, To Sister
    Leonor de la Misericordia, Soria; from Palencia, mid-January
    1582, 912; Letter 210, To Don Teutonio de Braganza; from
    Ávila, January 16, 1578, 512); *The Interior Castle* (6.1.7)

53. *The Interior Castle* (7.4.8); *The Way of Perfection* (4.4);
    Letters Letter 415, To Canon Montoya, Rome; from Burgos,
    about May 1582, 928; *The Way of Perfection* (4.5).

54. *The Interior Castle* (5.2.2-4); *Soliloquies* (6.1)

55. *The Interior Castle* (5.2.5-6); *The Interior Castle* (5.3.7); *Life*
    (4.10)

56. *Meditations on the Song of Songs* (1.9-10, 12); *Life* (11.1-2)

57. *The Interior Castle* (5.4.4; 7.2.4-5)

58. *The Interior Castle* (5.2.7-9; 6.6.4)

59. *The Interior Castle* (6.4.2-5); *Spiritual Testimonies* (12.6)

60. *Life* (29.13; 8.6) *The Interior Castle* (6.9.6)